JUSTICE AND WORLD SOCIETY

BY

LAURENCE STAPLETON

CHAPEL HILL
THE UNIVERSITY OF
NORTH CAROLINA PRESS
1944

COPYRIGHT, 1944, BY

THE UNIVERSITY OF NORTH CAROLINA PRESS

PRINTED IN THE UNITED STATES OF AMERICA
BY THE WILLIAM BYRD PRESS, INC.
RICHMOND, VIRGINIA

PREFATORY NOTE

I wish to thank several of my friends for reading the manuscript of this book and for the discussions I have had with them, especially Professor Grace de Laguna of the Department of Philosophy, Miss Bettina Linn of the Department of English, and Professor Karl Anderson of the Department of Economics, Bryn Mawr College; Professor Hans Kohn of the Department of History, Smith College; and Professor Marjorie Nicolson of the Department of English, Columbia University (who read the manuscript of chapters II and III). I am indebted to Mrs. Frances Frenaye Lanza for assistance with the translations from Vico.

LAURENCE STAPLETON

Bryn Mawr, Pennsylvania
December 17, 1943

CONTENTS

		PAGE
	Prefatory Note	v
I	Introduction	3
II	The Law of Nature	11
III	The Human Variable	33
IV	The Scope of Justice	78
V	The Ideal of Justice in Government	102
VI	Justice and Power	121
	Notes	131
	Index	145

JUSTICE AND WORLD SOCIETY

I. INTRODUCTION

The independence of America, considered merely as a separation from England, would have been a matter but of little importance had it not been accompanied by a revolution in the principles and practice of government. She made a stand, not for herself only, but for the world.—Thomas Paine, *The Rights of Man.*

The generation which commences a revolution rarely completes it.—Thomas Jefferson, Letter to John Adams, 1823.

THE SUBJECT OF THIS BOOK is the universal idea of justice, which at the time of the founding of the American republic was being studied and discussed as the Law of Nature. The debate over this concept is a kind of focus for the opposition between democratic and totalitarian beliefs.

When thinkers of the seventeenth and eighteenth centuries endeavoured to define liberty and justice in universal terms, they were supported by their understanding of what they called the Law of Nature. From the time of the Stoics this term had stood, in the political sphere, for an expression of the unity of mankind and the ability of men to determine by reason what is just. This was the kind of thinking which prepared for the Declaration of Independence with its premise that all men, by virtue of their humanity alone rather than of race or birth or social status, were entitled to life, liberty, and the pursuit of happiness. The Law of Nature, or as I have chosen to describe it, the universal ideal of justice, was the crystallization of belief in a power for good which transcended the barriers of race or nationality. It was held to be superior to the positive laws which might conflict with it and to set up a standard to which government and laws should conform. It furnished a basis alike for resistance to tyranny and for union in support of freedom.

The significance of such an ideal for modern times is clear. For it creates the basis for world understanding and for that sense of right common to all mankind without which no international organization can long survive. No matter what ingenious plans may be devised, if the informing spirit of justice is not present to illumine the mind and shape the will to act, there will be no peace.

But why should we, in thinking of world justice, study the sense of that ideal which the men of past generations agreed upon? We can, certainly, by our own thinking and our own experience, determine the general principles of justice. We tend to feel that we are more aware of the problems of world history or of the complexities of human nature than were, say, people of the eighteenth century. But the reason why we must re-examine the concept of the Law of Nature, of universal justice, is that if we think truly about this problem, we shall conclude that justice has always the same essential elements. If we were not to recognize and to understand the continuity of our thinking with that of the men who gave form to this ideal, and particularly with the democratic writers of the seventeenth and eighteenth centuries, we should suffer as it were a psychological breach in our development. This is particularly so because the grounds on which the Law of Nature was criticized in the nineteenth century, and which led to its abandonment as a working article of belief, are, as I hope will become clear, sources of confusing and weakening intellectual tendencies today. We cannot explore the meaning of natural law without considering the genesis and the implications of some of the ideas of opposite tendency.

The term "Law of Nature" is now an unfamiliar one. Inevitably, the early democrats who took it as their standard of justice expressed their thought in the idiom of their own time. They related this belief in justice to other beliefs not inherent in it or necessary to it—for example, they sometimes compared the Law of Nature to the axioms of mathematics. This was a natural result of the confidence in mathematical knowledge that followed upon the discoveries of Newton, but, like every other uncritical use of an analogy, it had strange effects. It led among other things to attempts to deduce by a priori reasoning from the general ideal of justice a host of particular moral obligations supposed to be binding upon the people of all countries.

This brought just criticism upon the concept of the Law of Nature. For it was easy to demonstrate that, as a matter of historical fact, all men did not share the same ideals, that there was a tremendous diversity in their customs and in their systems of property and personal relationship. It was also easy to show that each attempt to give specific embodiment to the Law of Nature, to enumerate the "laws" of which it was composed, varied somewhat from other similar attempts. Further, on account of changes in the general intellectual outlook of the times, and the growing popularity of new studies such as biology, the term "nature" came slowly to have a different connotation.

The movement counter to the Law of Nature and opposed to it I have called historicism—although other terms might be chosen to describe it. Chiefly, it consists in the belief that each people is so conditioned by its historical development as to be inherently different from the people of other nations, and hence unable to share with them common experience and common ideals. Regarding even injustice as an inevitable product of historical development, and denying to the individual any significance apart from his membership in a group, the complex of ideas that is here called historicism simultaneously cuts away the foundation of individual moral responsibility and makes impossible the world-wide sharing of an ideal of brotherhood.

Where people unconsciously began to accept ideas contrary to the Law of Nature, their democratic faith was to that extent weakened. As a rule democratic ideas were not openly rejected, but contrary and incompatible ideas grew up side by side with them. There was a slow change in the premises of political thought, particularly in Europe, without a realization of the consequences.

But ideas do have consequences. They are not merely weapons, they are expressions of what people believe to be true or false, and behaviour is largely governed by what people believe. At the time of the American Revolution a universal concept of democracy took shape. The issue was to lie between that concept, prepared for by discussion of the Law of Nature, and the counter-revolutionary trend of historicism.

For not only did the development of historicism weaken the understanding of democratic principles, but it became one of the chief roots of what we have come to recognize as the Nazi-Fascist ideology. (It is important to recognize that there is an affinity between ideas that tend to weaken and divide a democracy internally, and those that form the Nazi-Fascist program.) The main articles of the Nazi-Fascist creed are the positive value of struggle, hence of war; the supreme importance of the group, race, nation (often referred to as an organism), and the consequent insignificance of the individual; the superiority of irrational feeling, unanalyzable instinct, over reason; and the irresponsibility of authority. Each of these ideas separately, as well as all of them taken together, constitutes a denial of the possibility of a universal ideal of justice.

There have been studies of the philosophy of totalitarianism which find the chief source of these ideas in nineteenth century writers, chiefly in Darwin, in Nietzsche, and in Wagner. The thought of these men and of others was influential. But there has been some carelessness in describing the background. For one thing, there has been insufficient discrimination in the choice and isolation of the ideas to be described. Some of the ideas which the work of Darwin emphasized—the struggle for existence, to take an example—had been spread abroad before his time and had already influenced political thinking. Again, the word materialism has been used in describing the background of totalitarian ideas. But in Germany and Italy, at least, the precursors of totalitarianism conceived of themselves as revolting against materialism, and building up in opposition to it a "vitalistic" principle.

To investigate the whole history of the background of totalitarianism would be an immense labour. The phase of it with which I am concerned is only a part. It is not my intention to give a history either of the Law of Nature or of the ideas that ran counter to it. Nor am I concerned to expound in all its details the thought of the writers that I have chosen to represent the movement. I am concerned to identify and to interpret patterns of ideas. In attempting to show the implications for political thought of these opposed patterns, I have chosen writers to represent historicism who are not directly connected with Nazism or its immediate past. It should not be supposed that any of these writers would sympathize with Nazism; on the contrary, they would probably have detested it. I have chosen these writers partly because their work or their thought points to a wealth of material which it became the special interest of nineteenth-century writers to explore. From the beginning the process of investigation was accompanied by pseudo-scientific ideas which were uncritically adopted in other branches of thought, such as political and ethical theory.

Therefore, I have sought at the same time to put one main source of the Nazi ideology back farther than most recent writers have attempted to do, and to consider this pattern of ideas by itself before it was identified with the literary history of any one country. In short, I should like to show that certain ideas are inherently unsatisfactory as premises for political thought, not that they are unsatisfactory because they are connected with the Nazi movement. The prevalence of these ideas among Nazi writers is in my opinion a *symptom* of their deep-seated unsoundness.

But why did this philosophy gain ground? Was it not because of a certain immaturity, and inadequacy, in such concepts as that of the Law of Nature? In particular, was not the fundamental similarity of men to each other too simply stated? If anything was wrong with the eighteenth century ideal of brotherhood, *fraternité*, it was that it lacked concrete substantiation and was conceived in the absence of real knowledge. How are we going to account for the interplay between the many kinds of people, with the widely different circumstances of their lives, with their special needs and often peculiar habits—between all this diversity and the common understanding required for peaceful intercourse among them? This is the problem suggested by early attempts to explore what I have called the human variable.

After all, the kind of thinking which in its morbid and malignant stage has grown into the Nazi ideology had, certainly, a degree of plausibility. It did emphasize certain aspects of human life that had been given too little attention by earlier thinkers. In the form of relativism—the regarding of all phenomena and particularly of intellectual history as peculiarly a product of circumstance, to be explained in terms of its origins and antecedents rather than examined for its truth or falsity—it has had a powerful effect upon Western thought. It is difficult not to think that this movement has been more devastating in its effect upon the adherents of democracy than upon their opponents. For it has created a skepticism and disillusionment with the foundations of all belief, and with ideas that must be wholeheartedly accepted as true if democracy is to be thought of as in any way a fundamentally sound pattern of experience. Without belief in the value of individual experience, for example, and without belief in reason, it is hard to be a sincere democrat. But many intellectuals have cast doubt upon these ideas and have come to think of them merely as by-products of the rise of the middle class or of the eighteenth century *Zeitgeist*. In the *Dictionary of American Biography*, to take an instance, a writer refers to "such pieces of ritual as the preamble to the Declaration of Independence or the French Declaration of the Rights of Man and of the Citizen." That is an example of the effect of intellectual relativism. The writers and scholars who are inclined to think in these terms have rarely come to grips with the ideas to which they feel their thinking to be superior; they have merely succumbed to the cult of historicism and have cast aside profound ideas because they can detect remnants of a particular era of thought in the manner of their expression.

The term Law of Nature is outmoded and has connotations that are naïve, but its essential meaning is indispensable to democracy. The basic ideas of democracy are systematically connected, and it is possible to approach almost every concept through the analysis of another. But if the ideal expressed by the Law of Nature were not valid, there would hardly be a fundamental ethical principle for democracy to rest upon. The theory of the Law of Nature can be restated so as to meet the criticism levelled against it if it is clearly understood that what we are talking about is an ideal of justice in government. I call it an ideal of justice in government rather than simply an ideal of justice because it deals with the public relations of individuals and because it is not necessary to think of justice in government as being equal to absolute justice in a metaphysical sense. The principal problem to work out is the relationship of human differences to the common moral ground that we must share if we are to live together. I have tried to provide for the diversity of people within the terms of a universal ideal, and in this sense to extend the meaning of the concept of justice.

Our present situation again demands of us a conception of democracy that is universal in scope. The unity that comes from common opposition to a common foe is useful, but it is precarious, unless that opposition arises from the positive and constructive articles of belief for which we all stand, to which we hold ourselves responsible, and by which our actions are governed. Democracy is not aggressive, but it is inherently expansive. Where democracy stops, draws a line of colour or of nationality, it takes on the character of privilege. Believing that "the natural field of action for democracy is a field that embraces all mankind," I have tried to show the character of one of the oldest democratic ideas, the universal ideal of justice; to show the continuity between our way of thinking and that of the founders of America; and to anticipate the growth of this idea in a world society.

II. THE LAW OF NATURE

IN POLITICS, as in literature, there is no final appeal from the layman's point of view. Experts may classify and compare, but the very material of their investigation is given to them by the enterprise and imagination of uninstructed living men, uninstructed, that is, no matter how learned or how skilled in arts, as long as the net result of their endeavour lies in the future, as long as their experience has yet to run its course. No man could write about Shakespeare or the Declaration of Independence before Shakespeare and Jefferson themselves had written. The layman in his thought and his behaviour builds the stuff that the expert is to analyze. Indeed, the highest success that any expert can achieve is that his findings should enter the habitual thinking of his lay contemporaries or of future people, that the refined and tested conclusions of his labours should become again as raw material awaiting the research of others later on.

The inescapable truth of these maxims is borne out in literature by the supremacy of the common reader and in politics by the doctrine of consent. He who would bear witness against the judgment of the common reader will be heard at the bar which he condemns, while whoever assails the principle of consent must do so by force or leave his case to the verdict of others, and the choice of either alternative acknowledges the very power that it is sought to deny.

Is there not indicated here, beyond the statistics and the schools, a free margin of human intelligence from which the creative current flows, and for the service of which the statistics and the schools, the instruments and the measures, alone have been established? This, at any rate, is the kind of announcement given out—though in a different key—in that great nuclear concept of political thought, the Law of Nature. To the evolution of this concept Greek philosophers and Roman jurists and Christian theologians, commonwealth men and political philosophers and American revolutionaries, contributed their share. And at the moment when, in Europe, the concept of the Law of Nature seemed to disintegrate under the attack of the historical and geographical relativists, when it languished in anemia from the thin fare fed it by its codifying guardians, it had in America, in a changed form, a new birth. It is well worth while to seek out the kernel of this doctrine and to examine the notions that temporarily supplanted it—not for the sake of recalling ideas that have been, but asking, though the term Law of Nature as an effective article of belief has passed away, what constants in our own experience may be linked to these foundations.

The importance of the Law of Nature as a political concept is briefly this: that it sets up a standard of justice against which the actual practice of a given legal system or form of government can be measured. There never was a stage in its history when it did not have political implications. A doctrine that appeals from present imperfections to eternal right, from the actual to the possible, from the institution of slavery permitted in the Graeco-Roman world to the *natural* equality of all men everywhere[1]—such a doctrine tends always to reinforce the battles of conscience and freedom. So distinguished a jurist as Sir Frederick Pollock has told us that "the Law of Nature never ceased to be essentially rationalist and progressive."[2] And a historian of recent writings on the Law of Nature points out that even in the early stages of the concept there "lurked the germ of revolution, for on the basis of these precepts the whole structure of the state was subjected to criticism from a rationalist point of view."[3]

The idea of a "natural" law or of an ideal of justice valid in the whole community of mankind has had a long history, of which the general outlines are well known. Although in the writings of Plato and Aristotle there is much discussion of justice, and we owe to Aristotle the distinction between justice that is "natural" and justice that is merely conventional, or in accordance with the prevailing social customs, the idea was given its distinctive form by the Stoics. Their concern was not with the city-state, but with ideals broad enough to embrace the different nations brought together in the Alexandrian empire. But although a universal state provided the setting of Stoic ethical and political thought, their response to this challenge was not merely pragmatic. They tried to formulate a connecting link between their general conception of nature, as governed by reason, and the mind of man. "The fundamental principle of Stoic ethics and politics is the existence of a universal and world-wide law, which is one with reason both in nature and human nature and which accordingly knits together in a common social bond every being which possesses reason, whether god or man."[4] And since it was reason, rather than rank or status, nationality or wealth, which enabled man to recognize the unity between his own nature and the divine, there necessarily followed the beginnings of a notion of equality. In the possession of a common humanity, all men are equal. "Thus interpreted the principle of natural law becomes a recognition of intrinsic worth in human personality, with the necessary implication of equality and universal brotherhood."[5] This sentiment was before long to be powerfully reinforced by the teaching of the New Testament.

From the Stoics the idea of natural law was handed on to the Romans, and it became associated with the *ius gentium*, or law common to all nations, which the Romans had developed to regulate commercial dealings with foreigners who were not Roman citizens. In Cicero's great treatise, the *De Republica*, Stoic doctrines are summarized and brought into closer connection with the concerns of government. Natural law here is more than an object of contemplation for the wise man; it sets the standard to which actual laws and institutions must conform in order to deserve the name of justice. Following Cicero, Roman jurists like Gaius, Ulpian, and the compilers of the *Institutes of Justinian* took the Law of Nature as a basic premise, although they did not contribute to its theoretical development. From the Roman jurists the idea of the Law of Nature was absorbed by the Fathers of the church and was later to be enshrined in canon law.

In medieval times natural law was again the subject of philosophical debate, and its meaning was brought into conformity with the doctrines of the church. The great tradition of universal justice was widely disseminated throughout Europe. It was identified with the law of God, made known to man by reason. In this period, however, the political implications of the idea were dormant. In conflicts between the Empire and the Papacy, the Law of Nature was appealed to by both sides, and it was conceived that both Emperor and Pope were subject to it. If the question remained unsolved as to who had the right to interpret this ultimate law, the conviction grew that power whether ecclesiastical or civil was responsible to a criterion of justice that men could understand.

The Law of Nature could not enter into its own as a political concept until a historical situation arose in which the source of political obligation became a practical issue and the relation of the individual to government a matter of widespread discussion. From the sixteenth century on these questions were the center of debate on the Continent and in England, first because of religious differences within states, and later because of the encroachments of absolute monarchy. Natural law, especially in England, became an ally of the somewhat more domesticated "fundamental law," derived both from custom and from specific grants of privilege like Magna Carta. Again, the substance of the ideal of justice was left undeveloped, while the belief spread that arbitrary and willful authority, irresponsible and subject to no law, must be resisted and if necessary overthrown.

The service of Grotius, in his *De Iure Bellum ac Pacis* (1625), was to remove the idea of natural law from its dependence on theology. Although Grotius, perhaps happily, confused the Law of Nature and the Law of Nations *(ius gentium)*, he did at the same time demonstrate the possibility of a natural law freed from ecclesiastical influence and from dependence upon the church. Returning to classical sources and especially to Cicero, he described the Law of Nature as founded on reason and on the sociable nature of man. But in his treatment of the laws governing the relations of nations in war and peace, Grotius cited specific cases and examples which he tried to arrange in systematic form. This method of treatment no doubt influenced later writers like Pufendorf, Heineccius, Wolff, and Burlamaqui, who tried to extract a whole system of declaratory law from the general ideal of justice. It will be shown how such attempts contradicted the spirit of the Law of Nature and contributed to its eclipse. Yet the authors of these seventeenth- and eighteenth-century treatises, some of them men of practical experience in government, helped to create the unity of thought that was essential to the founding of democracy.

It will doubtless be granted that the doctrine of natural law as it was after the sixteenth century may fairly be considered without reference to the special problems of metaphysics, of theology, or of jurisprudence that cling to its earlier history.[6] If the tradition of the Law of Nature, looked at from a historical point of view, displays a remarkable continuity,[7] if the contributions of Stoic philosopher or doctor of the canon law have permanently enriched its composition, it remains true that the tradition lived because the main ideas were rethought in the present rather than rescued from the past. Locke, for example, derived his understanding of the Law of Nature from the main lines of descent, as his frequent references to Hooker show. Jefferson had not only Locke to lean upon but also his well read volumes of Wolff and Burlamaqui. Yet to Locke and Jefferson the laws of nature were self-evident not because a long line of history had made them familiar, but because they were working to establish standards for a type of government in which a man might engage himself, with satisfaction to his conscience, to follow decisions not solely of his own making. For this purpose the Law of Nature lay ready; if it had not already been elaborated, its essential elements must have been beaten out in some other form.

The version of natural law which was transmitted to the fathers of the American Revolution was the product of many minds and many countries: of Englishmen like Hooker, Coke, Algernon Sidney, and Locke; of the Dutchman Grotius; of the Germans Pufendorf, Wolff, and Thomasius; of the Swiss Vattel and Burlamaqui. But to Locke, more than to anyone else, we owe its abiding influence in America in the eighteenth century, for Locke clarified the connection between a universal concept of justice and self-government.

In the second, more important of his two political treatises, *The True . . . End of Government,* Locke is not primarily concerned with expounding the doctrine of natural law. But as the Law of Nature discloses the true purpose of government, so it throws direct light upon the way in which political power may be justly exercised. "The state of

Nature," says Locke—and by the state of nature he means only the absence of specific legal institutions, not the dim reaches of an improbable past—"has a law of Nature to govern it, and reason, which is that law, teaches all mankind who will but consult it, that being all equal and independent, no one ought to harm another in his life, health, liberty or possessions." There is an inherent value in human personality which it is the purpose of society in general, and more specifically of government, to make more secure. Apart from institutions which have set upon them the stamp of rank or office, *all men are equal*, not in ability or strength, but in the moral claim to respect and to a good life. When a government, by the use of arbitrary power or force, endangers the security and freedom which it ought to protect, it is no true government and man has no obligation to obey it. "The end of law," Locke says, "is not to abolish or restrain, but to preserve and enlarge freedom."[8]

Thus Locke works out more thoroughly than earlier writers had done the conjunction between justice, freedom, and the method of consent. Justice for all men, or the Law of Nature, gives government its end. The purpose of government is to preserve freedom and increase security. How is this to be achieved? By basing both law and the form of government upon the consent of the people. "The liberty of man in society is to be under no other legislative power than that established by consent in the commonwealth, nor under the dominion of any will, or restraint of any law, but what that legislative shall enact *according to the trust put in it*."[9] And here Locke makes a contribution of great value. He has shown the contradiction between justice and absolute monarchy. He goes beyond this to demonstrate the injustice of absolutism of any kind. Not only kings, but legislatures, are to have limits on their action. (This lesson Locke had learned from the Levellers, who were the first to suggest a bill of rights, or "reserved powers.")[10] The legislative power, whether placed in one or many, "is not, nor can possibly be, absolutely arbitrary over the lives and fortunes of the people. . . . Their power in the utmost bounds of it is limited to the public good of the society. It is a power that hath no other end but preservation, and therefore can never have a right to destroy, enslave, or designedly to impoverish the subjects. . . . Thus the Law of Nature stands as an eternal rule to . . . legislators as well as others."[11] Man cannot rightfully, whether individually or through his representatives, consent to tyranny. Not by a *single act* of consent, whether plebiscite or general election, is his future to be determined, but by the *continuing exercise* of consent, and all the conditions that make that possible. The state is not an end in itself. The life of man is an end. Here Locke has given the Law of Nature, or ideal of justice, a positive meaning for democracy.

Natural law as joined in seventeenth-century England with the tradition of self-government was no mere abstraction but a good summary of some very practical ideas about political relationships. So it was found to be in America. The American colonists could not have carried their breaking away from England to so great a conclusion if their general aims had not been agreed upon. In 1815, a Frenchman addressed to John Adams a query about the American Revolution. In reply, Adams asked, "But what do we mean by the American Revolution? Do we mean the American war? The Revolution was effected before the war commenced. The Revolution was in the minds and hearts of the people."[12] That agrees very well with Jefferson's comment that in the Declaration of Independence he did not aim at originality but at giving "the harmonizing sentiments of the day." Of these harmonizing sentiments, the general ideas of natural law were among the most powerful. For it was not on legal rights, varying from one colony to another, nor solely upon the "rights of Englishmen," that the colonists based their cause. "Without natural law there would have been no political theory common to all the colonies."[13] Charters varied, and there might be real doubt about the legal power of the English parliament in the colonies. But the concept of natural law helped to solidify agreement on the kind of government that was desired.

However important the effect of economic interest, the tradition of self-government in the colonies and the widespread belief in the rights of man had quite as much importance in determining the form of our government. Lawyers from Massachusetts bred up in Coke and Blackstone and well read in Locke, Grotius, Vattel found that their associates from Pennsylvania or Virginia had similar ideas. Jefferson in Virginia, John Dickinson and James Wilson in Pennsylvania depended upon natural law in their political writings no less than John and Sam Adams and James Otis in Massachusetts. Of Otis, John Adams said, "It was a maxim he inculcated in his pupils . . . that a lawyer might never be without a volume of natural or public law, or moral philosophy, on his table or in his pocket."[14] And at an early meeting of the Continental Congress, John Adams was anxious that natural law be advanced as the ground for the claims of the colonists, for it would prevent quibbling over legal documents different in different colonies and provide an understood basis of unity. Not without effect was Boston, as Professor Barker has remarked, "the home of natural law" as well as of other famous commodities.

To the effect of the natural-law doctrine in America we owe the universal aspect of American democracy, that "she made a stand not for herself only, but for the world."[15] If the franchise was still restricted, if slavery was still permitted to exist, the ideals of government written into the Declaration of Independence and the American Constitution looked toward a state of greater equality. And it is significant that the Law of Nature was a center of controversy once again in the Civil War, when it was vigorously attacked by the defenders of slavery.

We can now summarize the meaning of the Law of Nature as it emerged from two centuries of political discussion and entered its period of greatest practical effect. The moment of greatest influence for the Law of Nature coincides with the moment of least intellectual growth. It was powerful because it was generally accepted and understood; the vast elaborations of the treatises would soon be obsolete, but not the premises furnished to political thought. We must begin by analyzing the main elements on which most writers were agreed.

First among them was the belief implicit in the theory, whether in the form given it by the Stoics or the form in which it was received by men of common sense in the eighteenth century, that justice is not merely an ideal of man's devising but is a part of nature,[16] that is to say, is a structurally fundamental character of the given, or (from a slightly different point of view) a possibility in things that are. This was sometimes expressed by saying that the Law of Nature is established by God, sometimes by thinking of the Law of Nature as having over other forms of law a logical priority, in the manner of mathematical propositions.[17] The meaning of the word "nature" has varied in different periods and has been the source of much ambiguity. Later, the shift in meaning from nature as harmony and design to nature as struggle ("nature red in tooth and claw") had much to do with the eclipse of natural law in political theory. It would be desirable to drop the doubtful phraseology and to remember simply that it was an attempt to express faith in justice as an ideal of human relations.

Even without attending to the metaphysical implications of such a doctrine, its vitality as a foundation of political life must be clear to everyone. To say that justice is real is to claim, for example, that freedom in any place and at any time, with or without the guidance of past customs and traditions, will always be discoverable to be better than slavery. It is to know surely that, no matter how successful in any given period of history cruelty and wrong may be, the good and the equitable are there to be found again. And, finally, it is the only apprehension of things that gives any meaning whatsoever to choice or selection in human affairs. For if justice is not enough in accord with the character of experience to be possible of attainment, there is no use in striving for it; there is no merit in directing behaviour to fulfill the harmonies of an empty dream. Justice, in short, is nothing, or it is the hardest of realities.

The second great element in the construction of the Law of Nature is the recognition that justice is intelligible, that it may be rationally apprehended by the human mind. The Law of Nature is the Law of Reason. This is perhaps the most powerful article of political belief, from which all other claims to freedom stem. For the intelligibility of justice is what makes it most of man's concern; before justice man can never be passive. Authority may be obeyed, but justice must be sought and concurred with.

The supremacy of reason in the law does not exclude from consideration the sentiments and emotions, the needs and interests of mankind. It assumes, however, that man is capable of looking at his sentiments and emotions, his needs and interests, from a point of view that transcends immediate occasions. It assumes that man can do more than react; it assumes that he can objectify certain elements in experience so as to share them with other men. It also assumes that agreement, or peaceful behaviour among men, will be based on a common acknowledgement and understanding of these objective elements—in other words, that man is not merely capable of reason but that he values it in others. The criterion of intelligibility or rationality does not mean, then, that reason alone rules every other aspect of life; it means that what is arbitrary or irrational cannot be just. To decide to govern public affairs in a manner that is arbitrary or irrational is to omit or distort those objective elements that would enable others with a different approach to concur in the decision. We may say, therefore, that the notion of intelligibility includes the idea of common human qualities and impersonal communication concerning them.

But how shall we know those just laws which the natural reason of man approves? Shall we look for the kind of rule upheld by the common agreement of men everywhere? This is not an infallible procedure, for the majority of men may err; but over a long period it is a necessary one, for none but the majority of men can declare what best will suit mankind. Otherwise, justice would be in the custody of a few, it could never win moral obedience as distinguished from physical compliance, and it could not, on the human level, be reflective of reality. The notion of intelligibility leads directly to the notion of consent.[18] And implied in the notion of consent is the notion of individual judgment, inasmuch as there can be no consent without consultation. The decisions of all must be arrived at by means that insure the representation of each.

Finally, the Law of Nature is universal. No race, no nation, no group can claim a proprietary right in that sense of things which by definition transcends the local and the accidental, and conversely, no race, no nation, no group can be excluded from the natural community of all mankind. "Nor is it one law at Rome and another at Athens";[19] one law in Germany and another law in Poland. This element of universality in the natural law, its most vulnerable element, is vulnerable precisely because it is a truth of highest price. The universality of natural law is implicit in its being conceivable at all, in its being intelligible, and in its free appeal to consent; but the first three elements may appear to be present only to be negatived by the apparent breakdown of the fourth. Montaigne, wariest observer of variety, saw nevertheless that universality must be the criterion of justice:

> Equity and justice, if man knew of any that had substance and true being, would not be attached to the particular customs of this or that country. It would not

be from the caprices of the Persians or the Indians that virtue would take its form. . . . What kind of goodness is it that I saw yesterday held in honour, but that tomorrow shall no longer be so, and that is turned into a crime by the crossing of a river? What kind of truth is it that is hemmed in by these mountains, and becomes a lie in the world beyond them? [20]

But Montaigne professed to know no concept of justice some range of mountains did not bound. He pointed to the wide disparities of custom and behaviour in known societies, and to differences of opinion among philosophers as to what the Laws of Nature comprise, as evidence that no such universal laws could be discerned. This criticism, which anticipates that of the historical school, raises the question of the place and function of the whole concept we are discussing.

Now the description of the Law of Nature set forth above is of course a synthetic one, and it is meant, as has been noted, to apply mainly to the Law of Nature as a political rather than as a legal concept. But the synthetic picture differs little, I think, from the collective one that might have been pieced out of the definitions and postulates of Hooker, Grotius, Pufendorf, Burlamaqui, Heineccius, Wolff.[21] All these writers and indeed most of their precursors are agreed on the reality, universality, and rationality of the Law of Nature. They differ in their appreciation of the doctrine of consent, particularly as to the extent to which the common agreement of all nations is to be required as evidence that a supposed law of nature is in fact a law of nature.[22] They differ in attributing to the Law of Nature a source or ultimate principle—variously said to be sociability, or love, or reason, or happiness, or broadly the nature of man. The order, arrangement, and systematization of topics in the various writers differ in accordance with each one's cast of mind or the earlier models he may be following. These differences are unimportant. From Hooker to Jefferson there is hardly a writer who does not attribute to the Law of Nature the four elements that are here laid forth as being essential.

If our generalized version of the natural law is to be criticized, it should not be for arbitrariness, but it might be for omission. There is one phrase that occurs over and over again in the textbooks; the Law of Nature is said by almost all its learned expositors to be immutable, unchanging, constant. Is there, then, a fifth element that has been omitted?

If so, it is a serious omission, and one that must be justified. For the character of immutability was again one that exposed the Law of Nature to attack: as, in another context, the supposed immutability of the heavens had been called in doubt by the new astronomy of the sixteenth and seventeenth centuries, so the supposed immutability of the Law of Nature disintegrated under the revelations of the new geography and the new history of the eighteenth and nineteenth centuries. It would be unforgivable to leave out of the generalized summary of the Law of Nature its weakest prop.

Nevertheless, this omission can be justified. For from any abstract point of view, immutability can be subsumed under either the reality, that is the givenness, of the Law of Nature, or its universality. Immutability is simply universality in time. It is not properly speaking an independent element of the concept. Even the criticism to which the claim of immutability exposed the Law of Nature is of the same order as that evoked by its universality. The core of this criticism is the overwhelming impression of variety that is given by comparisons made in space and in time. A wider empirical knowledge and a deeper interest in social affairs made possible the demonstration that no body of law is in fact universally recognized, and that even within those portions of society where some body of law has long reigned, time has made room within the law for changed interpretations of the most fundamental institutions and human relationships–in, for example, the laws of property and of marriage. In this challenge to the Law of Nature and to the weak notion of immutability we are again presented with a question of function.

But eighteenth-century philosophers were not aware of the interest of this question. They had set up as a criterion of all law the benevolence of God or the humanity of man; they thought of the Law of Nature as intelligible, universal, and acceptable to free people. But they did not distinguish between that law as an identifiable body of rules of conduct and as a set of conditions for the foundation of just government. It is the latter notion alone that has strength, and the latter notion has survived at least in a practical form. For it is possible to say that if the Law of Nature was not wholly understood as a set of conditions or standards for law and political society, that is, nevertheless, how it was used. It was from the description of the general character of the Law of Nature, not its supposed content, that eighteenth-century ideas of right were derived. The political writers realized that it was a set of standards for the making of law by men, not the law itself that men would make. The Law of Nature in politics became the Rights of Man. It is because of this line of evolution that the Law of Nature in modern times is more fruitful as a political than as a legal concept.

This understood, it is clear that historical criticism can not reach the Law of Nature. For it was a doctrine never intended to have historical validity. Even when it was unfortunately associated with reference to an earlier condition of man, a State of Nature or a Golden Age, the intent was more to effect a criticism of the present by comparison with the prime uncorrupted possibilities that might be conceived, than to make assertions of fact as to the actual course of events in known times and places. The Law of Nature was not designed to be satisfactory on historical grounds, because even the best history would not have satisfied. What would satisfy, what was absolutely required, was a doctrine that would invest man's sense of himself with moral stability. Enlightenment on this scale alone would furnish guidance for man's relations with man.

Now in defending the omission of immutability from the generalized Law of Nature we have perhaps arrived at the question whether the omission of a principle of variability is not the more culpable. The Law of Nature, it is true, was designed to emphasize the qualities that men share in common. But the admission that the adaptability of man to his surroundings produces an abounding variety of local customs need not conflict with the recognition of those human needs and capacities that no environment can change or that a favourable environment would always encourage. Without some allowance for the factor of variability there could be only a very imperfect sense of unity; recognition of variability is therefore as important an element of the conditions for justice as any of the others.[23]

Certainly, the omission of a principle of variability from the prevailing concept of the Law of Nature was one of the causes that led to its overthrow. But unless the Law of Nature had been understood as a standard of justice, no principle of variability could have been incorporated with the rest. As long as the Law of Nature was thought of as in any sense descriptive rather than analytical, as long as it purported to list moral ordinances which could be shown to be universally respected, it was bound to be weakened as the sons of men became better acquainted with their mortal differences. The ensuing clash between uniformity and variety as norms of thought was in part simply the reflection in political theory of the rising of that complex phenomenon known as romanticism.[24] It was at the same time an intellectual revolt against the thinness of eighteenth-century Law of Nature doctrines and a bursting of the bonds, a cracking up of the old categories by the new, intrusive, undigested social facts that were the harvest of exploration, trade, travel, and the young sciences of botany and biology, so closely linked with geographical expansion.

It has already been said that the Law of Nature was not intended to be a historical or sociological doctrine as we understand such terms today. But, before the great westward expansion of European civilization which began in the Renaissance, it was not too far inconsistent with the known facts to suppose that some general laws of behaviour were everywhere acknowledged, some few virtues everywhere acclaimed. After the seventeenth century, however, the experience of sharp contrast between Western civilization and its newly discovered compeers was too striking to be ignored. Acquaintance with savages who had all the physical attributes of men but none of the habits or values of western Europeans was a new intellectual experience, and it took time for the full effect of this experience to show. We must also reckon with the effect of the *multiplication* of known societies—the sixteenth century knew itself, something of Islam and China, a little about Africa, and a little about the Indians of North and South America; the seventeenth century added a better knowledge of the Far East and of North and South America; the eighteenth century knew for the first time the peoples of the Pacific, and so on. The impact upon political and social thought of the discovery of what might be called alternative societies has never, to my knowledge, been adequately studied.[25] Indeed, it is a process still going on.

At first, the contrast between European society and the New World seemed refreshing. Delighted with their discoveries, anxious to present them in finest aspect, the voyagers and their chroniclers found not that the Law of Nature was unknown among the savages, but that it was their sole law and was more truly observed amongst them than among so-called civilized peoples. No anthropologists, the voyagers formed a very much oversimplified picture of a savage life uncorrupted by the frivolities of society, unfettered by the bonds of authority, untroubled by the perplexities of religion. In this first moment of enthusiasm and expansiveness, the Europeans let the contrast between their own and foreign societies point out to them their own shortcomings. As everyone knows, the travel books became the channel of much hard-hitting social criticism.

Now the Law of Nature itself was a weapon of social criticism, and when combined or confused with the idea of a State of Nature in which there was no institution of property, it became the vehicle of economic criticism as well.[26] As we read some of the writers of the sixteenth and seventeenth centuries we see that the tales of the voyagers temporarily reinforced the Law of Nature. Both furnished a standard by means of which existing abuses could be criticized and the ideal of a better social order be given substance. Professor Atkinson remarks that the thought of the virtues of man in the ancient world, in Turkey, the Indies, America, or China, "suggested to Montaigne the conception of a human nature far more perfect than the human nature manifested in France during the wars of religion."[27] This attitude comes out quite plainly in the bitter and powerful passage from the end of the essay, "Des Coches," the beginning of which is but a sample of Montaigne's indignation against the Europeans and his praise of the dignity of the Incas:

> . . . we have not brought [the new world] under our discipline by the advantage of our courage and natural strength, nor have we obtained it by our justice and goodness, nor subdued it by our magnanimity. . . . The astonishing magnificence of the cities of Cuzco and Mexico, and . . . the garden of that King, in which all the trees, the fruits and the herbs were excellently shaped in gold, according to the arrangement and size which they have in a real garden; as in his cabinet, were all the animals native to his lands and seas; and the beauty of their crafts-

manship in jewels, feathers, textiles, painting, showed that they were hardly inferior to us in industry. But when it comes to devotion, observance of laws, goodness, liberality, loyalty, candor, it served us well that we had less than they; they were lost by that advantage, sold and betrayed.[28]

This sentiment persists through the seventeenth century; in the popular mind the Law of Nature is increasingly identified with primitivism as a means of criticizing existing society. At the same time the Law of Nature in its intellectual growth is thinned out by its association with aesthetic and scientific uniformitarianism. After Descartes and Newton, the Laws of Nature were not merely thought of as intelligible, capable of being understood by reason, but as clear and self-evident, like propositions in geometry. Thus the Law of Nature became vulnerable on three grounds:

(1). Its association with the State of Nature. If it can be shown that primitive men with their ceremonies and taboos, their hierarchies and laws of kinship, are as fettered as European civilized men, then there is something like empirical evidence that the Law of Nature is not observed in the State of Nature. And if the two have been identified (Law of Nature = rules observed by men living without other prescription or rule of conduct), the conclusion will be that the Law of Nature is only a fiction.

(2). Its association with Cartesian-Newtonian rationalism. If it can be shown that men differ widely in their power to reason, that whole nations of men are incapable of grasping what to others are clear and self-evident truths, then it would seem that the Law of Nature is not the Law of Reason. (Nature is perhaps instinct or emotion rather than reason.)

(3). Its association with uniformitarianism. As soon as it becomes clear that the "fundamentals" of different societies are not the same, that even the desire to share in the same social ideals is lacking, the conclusion is drawn that all men are not equal, and that their differences are more important than their similarities.

Underlying all these criticisms and giving unity to them is the growth of the comparative spirit, from Montaigne to Montesquieu, from Vico to Herder, the rise of history and geography as modes of knowledge.

The atmosphere which led to the abandonment of the Law of Nature was prepared by the shock of the discovery in the Pacific of forms of culture more at variance with the culture of the West than any hitherto known. There began for some that change in the concept of human nature of which the reverberations still roll across the earth. The contrast between Europeans and more primitive peoples now was reversed, and was reckoned to the advantage of the Europeans. But the change in his attitude toward the savages led to a change in Western man's idea of himself.

Cook's voyages must, I think, be reckoned as a prime event in intellectual history.[29] The exploration of New Guinea, New Zealand, and Australia brought the first thorough knowledge of tribes living on the rim of humanity a life poor, nasty, brutish, and short—but not solitary. The romantic story of the Tahitian Omai (whom Cook brought home to England) is known to all, but it is deceptive. Cook's painstaking observation of ritual and superstition was in ill accord with the legend of a Golden Age. Cruelty and ignorance were the state of even the noblest savages, no longer to be hymned as "guiltless men that danced away their time." Among the litterateurs the cult of the noble savage perhaps still lingered. But among the founders of anthropology and ethnography, the physical makeup and customs of the savages aroused other emotions. It is interesting to observe that a hundred years later acquaintance with some of earth's poorest strangers could so powerfully affect Darwin:

The astonishment which I felt on first seeing a party of Fuegians on a wild and broken shore will never be forgotten by me, for the reflection at once rushed into my mind—such were our ancestors. These men were absolutely naked and bedaubed with paint, their long hair was tangled, their mouths frothed with excitement, and their expression was wild, startled, and distrustful. They possessed hardly any arts, and like wild animals lived on what they could catch; they had no government, and were merciless to everyone not of their own small tribe. He who has seen a savage in his native land will not feel much shame, if forced to acknowledge that the blood of some more humble creature flows in his veins. For my own part I would as soon be descended from that heroic little monkey, who braved his dreaded enemy in order to save the life of his keeper, or from that old baboon, who descending from the mountains, carried away in triumph his young comrade from a crowd of astonished dogs—as from a savage who delights to torture his enemies, offers up bloody sacrifices, practices infanticide without remorse, treats his wives like slaves, knows no decency, and is haunted by the grossest superstitions.[30]

The difference between Darwin and his precursors is mainly that by means of their accumulated evidence as well as by his own bent, his mind was prepared for the reflection, "such were our ancestors." Darwin's work completes the pattern woven by the three fields of knowledge that were to be the blending agents in social thought: history, geography, and biology. It is customary to date the rise of the historical school after the French Revolution, and to think of organismic concepts of the state as being a product of the nineteenth century. But the intellectual background for them had been prepared long before.

To take account of the new social facts reflected in the growth of the comparative spirit, the Law of Nature would have had to be revised. Its structural possibilities were not yet exhausted. But there could have been no revision at this time. Men always use new terms if they can to indicate the change or growth of their interests: otherwise they might not themselves be able to distinguish the new from the old. Indeed, the Law of Nature could only have been extended and improved by minds that had already digested and assimilated the very facts that broke it down. Only by introducing into the parent concept a principle to account for the new facts could it have been enriched and strengthened. To maintain the Law of Nature under the criticism of the historians and the recording in the travel books of the "dissonant harmonies of the children of men" would have claimed an almost metaphysical devotion. This was not to be expected from the eighteenth century.

If toward the end of the eighteenth century we turn our eyes on the condition of the Law of Nature concept, we observe that it is at a point of change, at a moment when, as has been said, its greatest practical effect coincides with its least intellectual growth. It will be the purpose of this essay to set forth some examples of the kind of political and social reflection which helped to interrupt the growth of the Law of Nature. These examples, taken from Vico, Buffon, and Herder, are to be looked at especially from the point of view of their interest in what I have called the human variable. We shall try in the end to determine in a speculative manner whether the successor theories made a better place for the human variable, and to explore the possibilities of a reconstructed Law of Nature.

III. THE HUMAN VARIABLE

Curiosity with respect to origins is for various reasons the most marked element among modern scientific tendencies. It covers the whole field, moral, intellectual, and physical, from the smile or the frown on a man's face up to the most complex of the ideas in his mind. . . . Character is considered less with reference to its absolute qualities than as an interesting scene strewn with scattered rudiments, survivals, inherited predispositions. Opinions are counted rather as phenomena to be explained than as matters of truth and falsehood. Of usages, we are beginning first of all to think where they came from and secondarily whether they are the most fitting and convenient that men could be got to accept. In the last century men asked of a belief or a story, Is it true? We now ask, How did men come to take it for true?—John Morley, *On Compromise* (1874).

> Are God and Nature then at strife,
> That Nature lends such evil dreams?
> So careful of the type she seems,
> So careless of the single life.
> —*In Memoriam*, liv.

SHOULD IT EVER FALL to the lot of some unhappy mortal to make an index or concordance of the papers and speeches of Adolf Hitler, there will be a very large number of entries under the item, "History." And this is appropriate. For "History," to Nazi and Marxist alike, is a convenient goddess; she is Fate in modern guise; she provides a stage for men to posture on and absolves her devotees of all moral responsibility to their contemporaries. This bitch-goddess "History" is not to be confused with the painstaking process by which some people (called historians) try to recover accurately the facts of what has happened in the past; on the contrary, the service of "History" by its political disciples sometimes seems to require that parts of the record of the past be changed or suppressed. There is, however, a convenient division of labour between this divinity and some of the scholars who are so confusingly called by a similar name. Some of them appear to have left it to her (or to anyone else who cares to usurp her office) to interpret what they have so painfully discovered. Although it is perhaps too early to understand the connection that may be suspected to exist here, is it too fanciful to suppose that some scholars were willing to abandon the richest fruit of their labours to the popular goddess of the laity, "History," because they themselves were occupied in the more esoteric worship of another goddess, "Science"?

It is doubtless a coincidence that an early follower of the cult of history named his principal work the *Scienza Nuova*. Giambattista Vico, a Neapolitan professor of rhetoric, was no friend to the physical science of his day. He was a critic of Descartes and an avowed follower of Bacon—and this is not surprising, for the rationalism of Bacon does leave more room for the assimilation of empirical evidence than the rationalism of Descartes. But Vico in his *Scienza Nuova* (1725; new eds. 1730, 1744), like Sir Thomas Browne in his *Pseudodoxia Epidemica*, followed Bacon's instructions to collect material for science without first freeing himself of the fixed ideas and prejudices that Bacon described as the idols of the mind. To Mr. Edmund Wilson,

"It is strange and stirring to find in the *Scienza Nuova* the modern sociological and anthropological mind waking amid the dust of a provincial school of jurisprudence of the seventeenth century and speaking through the antiquated machinery of a half scholastic treatise."[1] It may be doubted whether Vico was, in fact, as much of an apostle of enlightenment as Mr. Wilson implies. Brilliantly discerning in his contribution to the methods of historical research, enormously aware of the new sources of knowledge that lay in hitherto ignored social facts, Vico, in attempting to prove that myths were a species of history, made history a myth, and was the first of those who felt impelled to substitute for the ethical norm of universal nature the superstition of the inner development of the "folk."

This is not the place to try to do justice to Vico nor to attempt a systematic exposition of his rather unsystematic treatise. We are concerned only with the substance of ideas that tended to interrupt the growth of the Law of Nature concept. In order to identify opposing strands of thought, it is often necessary to isolate them from their context and to look rather to their implications and consequences than to the explanations by which an author may have reconciled them with his other ideas. Now first among the strands of thought opposed to the Law of Nature concept, and emphasizing the changing of standards rather than their universality, is surely that point of view which may be called historical relativism. The term "historical relativism" is seldom used and almost never defined by those writers who have done the most to establish its influence. The term is simply a convenient way of labelling the broad assumption that whatever form of authority or of custom or of law is characteristic of a given people at a given time must have been right for them at that stage of their history. The process of history thus becomes a kind of absolute which elbows out any moral judgment. Usually historical relativism, as thus roughly described, is associated with some kind of fatalism or necessitarianism which tends, especially in politics, to have a conservative or reactionary effect. In the eighteenth century especially, historical relativism is closely allied with the view that Professor Lovejoy has defined as the "principle of plenitude."[2] Whether we say, with Pope, "Whatever is, is right," or with Buffon, "Tout ce qui peut être, est," or with Hegel, "the real is the rational and the rational is the real," the effect of this principle as applied to human affairs is the same: the errors and injustices of the past are embraced equally with the hard-won truths; the same praise falls equally to tyrants and just men, that they have taken their part in the play; ignorance and cruelty are ranged equally with enlightenment and learning as simply the inevitable products of a time, a place, and a people.

This is not, indeed, a vantage point from which much of the motive force of human conduct can be discerned. It goes without saying that historical relativism, since it denies the fact or even the possibility of agreement among men of different times and places on the substance of right or justice, rejects any notion of a higher law. Historical relativism is essentially amoral since it will not recognize that moral judgment is a perception independent of history. The principle of historical relativism should, of course, be neither conservative nor the opposite, since it is a view that must welcome whatever happens. Criticism or even rebellion, when it appears, must logically be recognized as a constituent of the actual as surely as those conditions against which it is directed. Huey Long should have been the Kingfish of Louisiana, because he was the Kingfish; but it must have been right that he be assassinated, because he was assassinated. Nevertheless, with the partial exception of that branch of historical relativism exemplified by Marxism, the effect of the doctrine is more often than not either conservative or reactionary. It is used either to defend the status quo as "historical" and to reject change as a breaking with history, or to advocate some specious revival of a part of the past.

In truth, there can be no principle that is more useless in ethics or political theory than bare historical relativism. The omnipresence of historical necessity removes the need for obligation of any kind. But because it is difficult for human beings to shed all semblance of responsibility for their actions, it is usual for publicists of the historical school to take either the Past or the Future for their guide.[3] Again, the effort to realize justice in the life we know is sacrificed to some presumably superior heaven, and for this political eschatology, like the religious one, there have not been wanting men who felt called to be stewards and custodians.

The reactionary possibilities of historicism are shown by the ease with which it was woven into Fascist and Nazi ideology. Here, the role of historicism was to support extreme nationalism and to justify the denial of rights secured in modern times on the ground that they were inconsistent with an older "tradition" of German or Italian history. Historicism was invoked to deny the validity of progress, to "turn the clock back" and to defend an impudent revival of ancient wrongs, of tyranny and of suppression as methods of government. What was "revolutionary" in the Fascist-Nazi program was not historicism but the application of new techniques to the mobilization of power. Historicism furnished an appropriate apology because it had always been associated with opposition to liberal ideas.

Vico embraced the crude generality of wholesale historical relativism and made it the foundation of his work. His Utopia is the course of history itself. Vico's "true eternal republic," according to Croce, "is not the abstract state of Plato, but the course of history in all its phases, including the brutes at one end and Plato at the other. This is the 'republic of mankind,' the 'universal republic' (*generis humani respublica, magna generis humani civitas, respublica universa*) of which he means to investigate the 'form, ranks, societies, occupations, laws, crimes, punishments, and science of jurisprudence.' ... The 'great state of the nations founded and governed by God' is thus nothing else than History."[4]

In consequence, we are forced to accept all the events of history as being alike the work of Providence. "We may shudder at war, at the law of the stronger, at the reduction of the conquered to slavery ... but the society which expressed itself in these customs was necessary and therefore good."[5] Vico does not merely observe it to be a fact that the strong have conquered the weak; he is constrained by his a priori principles and his deification of history to give approval to aggression and conquest. Indeed, aggression or conquest is to him a kind of expression of divine providence; the stronger nations deserve to conquer the weaker. This suggests to him that there are two great truths of the natural order: "The first is that he who cannot govern himself should allow himself to be governed by others; the second is that the world is always governed by those who are by nature superior."[6]

Not only the might of the strong, but the frauds and deceits of the crafty or the superstitions of the credulous have their place. For example, Vico attacks the jurisconsults who saw in the harsher and more secret laws of ancient Rome before the Republic a product of the subterfuge of the nobles desirous of preserving their own power. He does not deny that secrecy was invoked to favour the interest of the nobles, but he considers that such customs are beyond criticism because they were appropriate to the time: aristocracy, the only government possible at that epoch, required such customs, and they were therefore justifiable because historically appropriate.[7] In similar vein he sees the hand of Providence in the use of the auspices by the Gentiles prior to the time when they were ready for the law of the Gospel:

... wherein we must admire Providence which, in the early times when the pagans did not comprehend reason ... permitted them to commit the error of substituting for reason the authority of the auspices and to govern themselves by their supposedly divine counsels.[8]

This line of reasoning would compel us to admire Providence for permitting human sacrifice by tribes which had no conception of the ideal of mercy or of the quality of human life.

There could be, for Vico, no general ideal of justice applicable to the different stages of man's history. There is only the sequence of development and the adaptation of customs at each level to the prevailing state of culture. He sometimes borrows the expression "natural law" to signify the historical process according to which, as he thinks, man in the end realizes his true nature.[9] But since all steps in this development are to be regarded as equally a part of the plan of Providence, there is no political ideal by which man may hope to rise above arbitrary power, barbarism, violence. That must be left to the unfolding of time. The process of history has been substituted for the concept of justice as an aim for human effort.

It is in his discussion of the three types of jurisprudence which correspond to the three principal stages of human development that Vico's approach to the philosophy of law is revealed. Michelet pointed out that, for Vico, "la jurisprudence varie selon la forme du gouvernement."[10] It would perhaps be more accurate to say that, in Vico's theory, the character of law as well as the form of government corresponds to the prevailing state of culture: in the age of the gods, a divine or theocratic government is supported by divine jurisprudence *(diritto divino)*; in the age of heroes an aristocratic government corresponds to heroic jurisprudence *(diritto eroico)*; in the age of men, a monarchic or republican type of government is upheld by humane jurisprudence *(diritto humano)*.

Now in the idea that positive law varied in different countries and in different epochs there was nothing new, even if the course of those changes and the reasons for them had not received sufficient attention. Indeed, recognition of the variability of positive law is an essential part of the Law of Nature theory, which does not deny that positive laws vary, but emphasizes that this variability is in sharp contrast to the unchanging criteria of justice that reason allows men to understand. The Law of Nature leaves room for the alteration of civil laws and recognizes that law as a mechanism of social life must change so as to take account of local conditions or to measure by local standards where they do not conflict with justice. But it is the merit of the Law of Nature that it asserts that the law of the tribe is not identical with justice, that no local law can be so absolute that appeal may not be taken to the general sense of justice of all mankind.

It is this idea, the idea that is the core of Christianity and of modern democracy, that Vico has cut away at a stroke with his theory of the three kinds of jurisprudence. But there is in his work no adequate examination of the Law of Nature, nor are grounds given for its rejection. He could, for example, have maintained that man has attained the full measure of his nature only by slow development, that there were stages in human history when the Law of Nature could not have been understood, that the Law of Nature must be interpreted as an ideal, a permanent possibility, rather than as a transcendent obligation binding even on the ignorant. At one moment it seems that Vico might have approached the Law of Nature in this light, for he sees in the Age of Men an era of gentle and peaceful customs, of humane jurisprudence, ruled by a form of government in which "through that equality of human intelligence which is of the essence of human nature, all men are made equal by the law."[11] In this state all men are born equal, he adds, as in a monarchy, where all men are equally subjected to the law! There is something like a notion of progress in Vico's thinking, but it is nullified by his setting the sequence of development in an unending cycle, in which progress upward from sensuous knowledge and violence to reason and equity is succeeded by a downfall of civilization in the "barbarism of reflection"; this is followed by a subsequent period of new growth that seems to require a renascence of violence and of the "heroic" life. Like all such patterns of history, including Spengler's, Vico's theory of cycles is in its political implications reactionary and fatalistic.

We may notice, too, that Vico is not without a special sympathy for the heroic age and for the primitive in general. It is this quality which leads Croce to remark that his thought "was entirely dynamic and revolutionary"[12] and which, doubtless, has made Vico popular among Italian sympathizers with fascism. Even the myth of "young" nations is not lacking:

> And this must be the reason why the Romans were the heroes of the world; for Rome subdued the other cities of Latium, thereafter of Italy, and finally of the world at a time when her heroism was that of youth, while the other peoples of Latium, from whose conquest came all the grandeur of Rome, must have begun to age.[13]

Vico's interest in the primitive is related to his taste for the imaginative and poetic as distinguished from the general or abstract. Croce indeed calls this an interest in the "individualising forms" in contrast to the interest of Descartes in the "universalising" forms. But this is a separate topic and deserves separate treatment.

Like most thinkers of his age, Vico felt the need of establishing some universal criterion of humanity, some distinguishing feature or quality that would allow him to think of the world of men as one. But he did not find this universal criterion in right reason or in common sense as it was understood by other thinkers of the time, to whom common sense meant judgment. We may take Descartes as the classic expositor:

> Good sense is of all things in the world the most equally distributed ... the power of forming a good judgment and of distinguishing the true from the false ... is by nature equal in all men.... For as to reason or sense, inasmuch as it is the only thing that constitutes us men and distinguishes us from the brutes, I could fain believe that it is to be found complete in each individual.[14]

A similar belief in the validity of reason and in its being the distinguishing mark of humanity was written into the natural-law theory from the time of the Stoics, to whom, however, the rule of reason was not achieved without effort. This belief, the heart of democracy as well as of the natural law, was set aside by Vico in favour of a pre-romantic notion of collective consciousness which he called *senso commune*, a "judgment without reflection" felt by an entire class or an entire nation.[15] Thus the principle of unreflecting collective feeling is substituted for the principle of the general consent of individual thinking minds.

In the formulation of his social philosophy, there is no doubt that Vico drew on ideas derived from the travel books as well as from his historical and philological studies. To this source is to be attributed his interest in what we may call folk customs. In consonance with the *senso commune*, which unerringly knows the human needs that are the sole source of natural right, all nations may be observed to have arrived at the possession of three customs: all have a religion, all have some form of solemn marriage contract, and all practice burial of the dead.[16] He turns to the accounts of the voyagers to bear out his contention that all peoples have some belief in immortality:

> And that such was also the feeling of the barbarians of the ancient world is proved by the people of Guinea,

as Huegues Linschoten witnesses, and those of Peru and of Mexico, as Acosta tells us in his *De Indicis*, and the natives of Virginia, according to Thomas Harriot, and those of New England, according to Richard Whitebourne, and of the kingdom of Siam, as we know from Joseph Schouten.[17]

Vico's emphasis on folk customs is a clear example of the influence, not to be fully felt until the nineteenth century, of the growing interest in primitive forms of society. In particular, the discovery of the similarity of certain ritual practices among all primitive groups and of the forms of tribal organization led to an increased stress on religion and the family as the basic or originative factors in political or social life. To Vico, the State of Nature "was really the same as the state of families."[18] The old State of Nature, as it appears in the familiar contract theory, is discarded as being too anarchic and individualistic.

In consequence, the Law of Nature as heretofore understood is undermined—not because the Law of Nature and the State of Nature are logically related but because they are associated in people's minds; in the State of Nature the Law of Nature was said to rule and the political contract was said to originate. When the State of Nature was no longer understood as a juridical abstraction, and was no longer associated with the Golden Age but equated with the actual state of affairs to be observed among primitive tribes, and when these primitive tribes were found to lack all knowledge of any social contract and to be governed by inherited traditions and customs rather than by rational laws, the inference was plain that the Law of Nature and the political contract must be idle fancies. Inevitably the effect of this stress on religion, custom, and the family as the true foundation of social life was a deprecation of individual choice and of the role of reason in human affairs.

Throughout the *Scienza Nuova* there is a strong tendency toward anti-rationalism. This is further manifested in Vico's curious distinction between certitude and truth. Certitude alone is possible to men. The surest knowledge, Vico holds, is the creator's knowledge of what he has made; or, as Croce expresses it, the main principle of Vico's epistemology is "that the condition under which a thing can be known is that the knower should have made it, that the true is identified with the created, *verum ipsum factum*."[19] The study of the natural sciences can never lead to certain knowledge, since the world of nature was not made by man. Only God, the creator of the natural world, can have certain knowledge of physical phenomena. But the social world is of a different order. For, as Vico tells us in an oftenquoted sentence, man is the creator of the social world.[20] Civilization is his work; the manner of its creation is reflected in his own soul, and it is possible "to discover its principles in the very transformations (*modificazioni*) of the human mind."[21] Without entering into the mysteries of the conversion of the true with the created as discussed by Croce, it is perhaps permissible to comment on the more obvious implications of this approach to the study of society. With the problems in methodology presented by Vico's distinction between the natural and the social sciences we are not concerned, nor with the faint anticipations of Kant to be found in his work. What does matter is his sympathy for the subjective, and his feeling that the presence of subjective attitudes in the study of social data, far from being a handicap, is a positive advantage. There is, so to speak, a kind of affinity between the prominence given to the *Volksgeist* by writers of the historical school and this preference for the subjective.

No doubt Vico's distrust of reason may be partly explained as a phase of his reaction from Descartes and his feeling that clear and distinct ideas, far from being evidence of truth, are evidence of incompleteness. It is thoroughly understandable that there should have been a reaction against mechanical rationalism and that Vico especially, a student of rhetoric and of poetry, should have been sensitive to the value of imaginative and symbolic forms of experience. But he goes beyond the stage of criticism to the point where he reveals a predilection for the non-rational, if not for the irrational: "the more vigorous the imagination," he says, "the weaker the faculty of reasoning."[22] Because of his sympathy for the imaginative and poetic he is moved to attack the methods of science. He is not the first who has failed to surmount the obstacles raised by the opposition of science and poetry. The fundamental question involved, that of the problem of knowledge in art, is a highly interesting one although usually, from Plato on down, obscured by the assumptions concealed in the form of the question asked. Vico's contribution to this problem is, in any case, of little value. What is significant for our purpose is that his appreciation of the truth in poetry led him to wish to strip science of the ambition for truth.

What we are dealing with here is essentially a confusion of material and method—a confusion which, if I may be permitted to say so, Croce shares with Vico. Thus Croce believes Vico's discovery of the importance of myths is "another aspect of [his] vindication of the non-logical forms of knowledge against the intellectualism which denied them and merely represented them either as artificial forms or as due to supernatural causes."[23] Now the point here is that the "intellectuals" were wrong only because they had not observed the *fact* that myths may be shown to be primitive attempts to construct history or otherwise to deal with actual experience. The discovery of the value of myths as material for study does not for a moment mean that this study can best be carried on by the processes of thought that shaped the myths. Then again, Croce asserts that a merit of Vico's theory is "the vindication of the world of intuition, empirical knowledge, probability, and authority."[24] This seems a most confused statement. To point out relevant facts *about* traditions, myths, or forms of authority, is to open a field for empirical inquiry, but the inquiry itself, if it is to be truly empirical, cannot be conducted by means of cloudy intuitions, or be limited by traditions, or be guided by obedience to authority. Clear and distinct perceptions may not be an automatic guarantee of truth, but that does not mean that we can rely more securely on obscure and indistinct ones, however important may be the material they contain.

Thus in Vico's confused thought there are two strains. He is first of all a critic of the abstract rationalism of his time and a discoverer of new sources of knowledge which should enrich man's comprehension of the world. He saw in ancient myths and religious cults, in poetry, in folklore, and in linguistic changes, in the study of ancient coins and monuments, in the comparative study of the history of law and of social institutions, rich material for history and for still unnamed subjects like anthropology and sociology. He gave a magnificent example of his own method in expounding the theory that Homeric poetry was not the work of one man but the collective expression of the whole Greek people. But—and this is the opposing strain—in pointing out these misunderstood, ignored, or undervalued elements in the history of the past, Vico revealed certain predilections and sentimentalities of his own. He not only points to the wealth of social knowledge in the neglected study of traditions and of the forms of authority that have affected people's lives, but he expects that this very study should be coloured by a positive attitude of appreciation. He extols the *sapienza volgare* in which the wisdom of ancient times is embedded, and he deprecates the nascent light of reason by which that of modern times is being clarified. In his vindication of myths as collective apprehensions of reality there is perhaps a hint that all collective apprehensions of fact will be of the nature of myth—the conclusion of Sorel and of the National Socialists.[25] All through Vico's work there is this confusion between the new sources of knowledge that he must be praised for uncovering, and the method of studying them, which in his mind is shadowed by his sentimental affection for the primitive and heroic. It is the tragedy of one powerful aspect of the romantic movement in culture, of what G. A. Borgese has called the second Counter-Reformation, that having discovered the omissions of mechanical rationalism, having discovered that the conditions of the development of man and of society did not correspond to any known scheme, having indicated the place for anthropology, psychology, the history of law, these thinkers, Vico among them, resorted to a counsel of despair in the only power that could conduct or profit by such investigations—the human mind.

Almost everyone who has ever written about Vico has pointed out that his work had to wait until the nineteenth century for recognition. It had to wait, really, until there was preparing, chiefly in Germany, an intellectual milieu in which the myth of History was supreme. Perhaps the writers of the so-called historical school were not only fit audience for Vico, but in a sense an audience he had helped to make. This much we know—that Goethe received a copy of the *Scienza Nuova* in Naples in 1787 and lent it to Jacobi in 1792; that Herder first mentions Vico in 1797 but (in my opinion) shows evidence in the *Ideen* of having read him earlier;[26] that Niebuhr was acquainted with Vico and recommended him to Savigny although he does not mention Vico in connection with his studies in Roman history, nor does Wolf acknowledge any debt to Vico for suggestions leading to his own theory of Homeric poetry. The *Scienza Nuova* was translated into German in 1822 by W. R. Weber.[27] Not, however, the tenuous strands of influence, but the broad pattern of ideas wrought into consciousness from similar sources of experience and by similar lines of reasoning, must account for the phenomena of intellectual history.

Finally, in weighing Vico's contribution to the picture of

the human variable, there is perhaps some need to emphasize the obvious fact that his relativism, like that of most philosophies of history, calls attention to the variation of groups of men, not of individuals. A little reflection will quickly show that an idea of man as everywhere the same, such as that shared by most thinkers of the Enlightenment, is quite compatible politically with fervent belief in the rights of the individual. For no man's claim to existence and to development is more profound than that of another, and each deserves the independence and the freedom which is a necessity to the "nature" of man as such, to the kind, man, to which all belong. There is, in addition, an encouragement of sympathetic feeling toward others as sharing the same nature with one's self, the ideal that is expressed in the word brotherhood or fraternity. Conversely, those philosophies which most strongly assert the unlikeness of men living at different times or in different quarters of the globe, tend to be affiliated with political notions that are designed to justify the imposition of uniformity on large units and to exclude others from the forcefully unified group. This is because it is not the variation of individuals that is stressed but the variation of tribes or nationalities. Vico, of course (in spite of his fondness for Roman history), cannot be regarded as a nationalist. Where, however, he is concerned with the variability of standards, it is not the variation of individual but of tribal or national standards that he considers. And where he seeks for a principle of unity in history, he is content to end his search with the similarity of instinct or of primitive traditions and to make of the *Volksgeist* a criterion of humanity.

So far we have been concerned with the theme of variability as it appeared in the philosophy of history. As it entered political thought, consciousness of variation owes more perhaps to biology or "natural" history than to any other source. A writer like Buffon was not in the least concerned with political ideas. He is neither a supporter nor an opponent of the Law of Nature theory that has been sketched in the first part of this study. But he did as much as anyone else in the eighteenth century to give an entirely different meaning to the concept of nature. Not that, of course, there were not evolutionists of one sort or another long before Buffon, as well as several contemporary with him. The publication of the *Histoire Naturelle* (1749-1788) is, however, a kind of landmark. Certain ideas that were to play a considerable part in the political thought of the nineteenth century have here an early expression, and it is all the more valuable to be able to detect their outlines before they have been filled in by the details of another subject. The gradual, almost unconscious assent to these ideas is one among the many causes of the lapse into disfavour of the Law of Nature. In addition, Buffon's work spread before a wide audience the implications as to the nature of man latent in these new studies. "Avant lui, *l'histoire naturelle de l'homme* n'existait pas. On étudiait l'homme individu, pas l'homme espèce."[28]

Rousseau has left an amusing reminiscence of how natural history succeeded mathematics and physics as a tonic to his imagination:

> Tantôt avec Leibniz, Malebranche et Newton,
> Je monte ma raison sur un sublime ton,
> J'examine les lois des corps et des pensées;
> Avec Locke je fais l'histoire des idées;
> Avec Kepler, Wallis, Barrow, Raynaud, Pascal,
> Je devance Archimède, et je suis l'Hôpital.
> Tantôt à la physique applicant mes problèmes,
> Je me laisse entraîner à l'esprit des systèmes:
> Je tatonne Descartes et ses égarements,
> Sublimes, il est vrai, mais frivoles romans,
> J'abandonne bientôt l'hypothèse infidèle,
> Content d'étudier l'histoire naturelle.[29]

The very phrase, natural history, throws another emphasis on the meaning of nature, which seems no longer a law, a standard, or archetypal idea, but a mysterious, all-enveloping complex in which the phenomena of growth and variety are the most striking. In the introductory essay, "De la manière d'étudier et de traiter l'Histoire Naturelle," Buffon discusses the conditions imposed by the fullness and complexity of the phenomena of nature. At first, he says, it may seem possible to schematize observations according to some simple formula or to map out some regular plan that leads through the mighty maze. That is an illusion. "We naturally tend to imagine in everything a kind of order and uniformity; and if one examines the works of nature only casually, it does appear at first glance that she has always worked on the same plan."[30] But the attempt to build systems on the abstractions conceived by our limited minds serves only to show "the inclination men have to seek for resemblances in objects the most dissimilar, regularity where variety is the rule, and order in things where only confusion is perceived." When we have carried out long and painful observations without being prejudiced by abstract systems, we are then struck by the abounding variety of nature—"as much surprised by the variety of design as by the multiplicity of means of execution."[31]

To the concept of variety as synonymous with nature should be added the force that produces variety, that of organic growth. The notion of growth or struggle is not so highly developed in Buffon as it is in Darwin. It comes out most strongly in his discussion of the organic particles by means of which "earth is made into plants, earth and plants are made into animals, and earth, plants, and animals are made into man."[32] The vital processes of nature are "the faculties of growth, development, reproduction, and increase in numbers."[33] But the world is crowded with an infinite number of beings each trying to develop itself. From this sense of fullness and crowding, Buffon (and other naturalists) arrived at the idea of the struggle and competition of creatures with each other. This did not pass into general currency before Darwin: in fact, I am inclined to think that the idea of competition had first to become generally familiar by means of its popularization from another source.[34] Nevertheless Buffon did anticipate Malthus and Darwin in the idea of the struggle for survival, as the following passage clearly shows:

> Thus, violent death is a process almost as necessary as the law of natural death. They are both modes of destruction and of renewal; the one serves to continue nature in perpetual youth, the other to maintain the order of her productions and to limit the number of species. Both are effects depending upon general causes. Every individual born dies at the end of a period of time. If he is prematurely destroyed by others, it is because he was superfluous. . . . What a swarming of numbers among [certain] animals! If they were not in large part destroyed by others, what would be the effect of this boundless increase? . . . And since one may say the same of all the other species, it is necessary, then, that some should live on the others. It follows that violent death among animals is a legitimate, an innocent process, for it is founded in nature, and creatures are born only under that condition.[35]

Now one result of the study of natural history is the perception of man as a part within nature, no longer a rational being who by virtue of his reason partakes of the universal harmony, but merely a part included within a whole to which it is subordinate. To be sure, Buffon in his essay "De l'Homme" remarks that it is only the study of the exterior part of man that belongs to natural history, but that the interior part of man, the soul, marks him off sharply from the animals and other living things. We may note, however, that the little preface which deals with "l'homme intérieur" occupies about ten pages, while the rest of the treatise, which in effect deals with man as a species, occupies nearly four hundred pages. In the essay "De la manière d'étudier et de traiter l'Histoire Naturelle," Buffon declares:

The first truth that emerges from a serious study of nature is perhaps a humiliating one for man: namely, that he ought to place himself in the class of animals, which he resembles in all that is material in him. Even the instinct of animals will perhaps appear to him more reliable than his reason, and their industry as more admirable than his arts.[36]

Like Blumenbach and like Herder, Buffon considered that all men belonged to one great family or species.[37] He thought variations in colour and in physical appearance generally were not primary but were produced by differences in climate, nutrition, and customs:

> ... man, [whose skin is] white in Europe, black in Africa, yellow in Asia, and red in America, is nevertheless everywhere the same man, the colour of his complexion changed by the climate.[38]
>
> One could not say that men such as those of the Mariana Islands or of Tahiti or of the other little islands in the middle of the ocean, at such great distances from all inhabited land, are not nevertheless men of our species. For in mating with us they can produce offspring [*produire avec nous*] and the small differences that we notice in them are only minor variations caused by the influence of climate and of diet.[39]

Nevertheless the vivid descriptions of the varieties of mankind to be found in the writings of Buffon and of other naturalists contributed to a habit of thought which slowly substituted for the idea of one universal human brotherhood a picture of groups of men scattered over the face of the earth, each with its own appropriate laws and customs, and each adapting itself even in appearance, as did the animals, to its local habitat. Thus although Buffon and Herder, for example, were emphatic believers in the unity of man, they and the other speculative thinkers of the natural-history school prepared a canvas which only a few swift strokes could easily distort to serve the purpose of racists and nationalists in the succeeding century. Their work must therefore be regarded as among the sources of the ideas that for a time supplanted the concept of the Law of Nature with its fundament of human equality.

For a student of authoritarian doctrines of government it is of great interest to find, as a concomitant of these early speculations in biology and anthropology, the same notion as that given by the fascists, even in their official documents, to justify the denial of all individual rights. This is the notion that it is the life of the species (or later, race) that counts, not the life of the single member.

> An individual, of whatever species he may be, counts for nothing in the universe; a hundred or a thousand individuals still are nothing. Species are the only beings in nature: beings as lasting, as ancient, as permanent as nature herself. To judge them more accurately we should not think of them as a collection or a series of similar individuals, but as a whole independent of number and of time, a whole that is always living, always the same, a whole that counts as one in the works of creation and therefore makes only a single unit in nature.[40]

This pronouncement as to the permanence of species may seem a bit strange in view of Buffon's firm rejection of all aids to classification in his attack on the Linnaean system, and his own preference for *les nuances*. Earlier, he had written, "the larger the number of classifications one sets up among natural phenomena, the closer one approximates to the truth, since really only individuals exist in nature; genera, orders and classes exist only in the imagination,"[41] and "Nature knows neither class nor genus, she is made up of individuals alone. These genera and classes are the fabrications of the mind; they are only conventions."[42] It was hardly possible, however, to attempt the study of natural history without resorting to the useful notion of species, however cautiously, and thus we find Buffon in "De la manière d'étudier et de traiter l'Histoire Naturelle" writing that "the history of an animal ought to be not the history of an individual, but that of the species to which the animal belongs."[43] In the "Comparaison des animaux et des végétaux" which forms a part of the general introduction to the *Histoire des Animaux*, Buffon states that however remarkable the individual may seem, "it is in the succession, in the renewal and in the persistence of species, that nature appears entirely mysterious."[44] By the time he wrote "De la Nature Seconde Vue" he was bold to say that the individual is nothing, and that species are the only beings that exist for Nature. Whether or not a real change took place in Buffon's thinking matters little in this connection; he has given us a clear expression of the anti-individualistic view which we rightly associate with the effect of biological analogies on political thought.

Then Buffon goes on to argue that the minute we substitute the point of view of the species (later read "group" or "race") for that of the individual, our standards of value change. When, for example, a human being contemplates the renewal of life in the spring after the inertia and frozen deadness of winter, he suffers an illusion of perspective:

> ... these ideas of renewal and destruction, images as it were of life and death, however grand and general they appear to us, are only of individual and particular meaning. Man looks upon nature from the perspective of an individual. But the being whom we have supposed to be a representative of the species thinks more greatly and more generally. In that destruction, in that renewal, in all the successions of nature, he sees only what is permanent and enduring. A season of one year is to him the same as the season of the year before, it is the same season for centuries back, and the thousandth animal in the order of generations is the same to him as the first.[45]

It takes but little imagination to translate the harmless image describing the difference between man's temporal perspective and that of Nature, into the idea that the individual is similarly deceived in surveying the wars and cruelties that trouble the earth, since from the point of view of the succession of beings, of the race or species, evil and destruction may be productive of good. This, indeed, can be the background of a heroic view of life.[46] But it can also be the weapon of cruelty and tyranny, claiming exemption from justice on the ground that the injuries and wrongs inflicted in the present will be justified "in the long run." Intrinsically, this doctrine is the simple opposite of the parable of the good shepherd; reversing the parable it declares that it matters little if the one sheep be lost, so the ninety-and-nine are left to represent the species. To make the anticipation of Darwin complete, Nature is presented as indifferent to the struggle between species and to the domination or extinction of one by another.

> ... the silk-worm, so precious to man, is to nature nothing but a mulberry grub. If that luxury-producing grub disappears; if other grubs devour the grass intended to fatten our cattle; if still others consume our corn before the harvest; if in general man and the higher species are starved out by lower species; nature is no less complete or less full of life. She does not protect some species at the expense of others. She supports them all, indifferent to numbers where individuals are concerned, seeing individuals only as successive impressions of the same stamp, fugitive shadows of that body which is the species.[47]

In conclusion, it must not be forgotten that Buffon is not in any way directly concerned with legal or political questions, but his work is an example of the sources from which views antithetical to the Law of Nature were drawn. It is worth repeating that the main works of the Law of Nature were not disabled by direct criticism; but when a quite different set of premises about the nature of man and about man's place in nature had moved into people's minds, the

Law of Nature was held to be superseded. And these views, so ambitiously spread out in the more "scientific" political treatises of the nineteenth century, were usually taken, by the most uncritical kind of analogy, from the biological sciences or rather from speculations about them. Because it may be instructive to identify the bare bones of some of the mysteries that now appear clothed in the flesh of power and propaganda, it has seemed worth while to include Buffon in this discussion.

The ideas that in Buffon and Vico are but symptoms and anticipatory stirrings of a marked change in the premises of European political and social thought are collected in strength in Herder's *Ideen zur Philosophie der Geschichte der Menschheit* (1784-1791).[48] Herder combined in a broad synthesis the relativism of history with its stress on custom and tradition and the emphasis on variety, growth, and struggle derived from the budding sciences of botany and biology. He brought these concepts of romantic thought sharply to focus on the question of man's place in the scheme of things. In many respects a thinker of the Enlightenment, Herder's aim was to preserve the possibility of regarding man as essentially one, through past and future, through regions civilized and uncivilized, through episodes of his history tragic or noble, pitiful or grand. He managed to do this by reducing the quality of the universal attributes of man from conscious functions, like reason, to unconscious adaptations to the process of living, like "organic forces" or primitive traditions of the folk.

The great age of specimen collecting which laid the foundations for the study of botany and comparative anatomy had progressed a long way from the period in which a Kaffir's skull or the skin of a bearded Moor was a prime exhibit in someone's cabinet of rarities. The eighteenth century saw the establishment of fine zoological gardens in London, Paris, Stockholm—and although there never yet has been a man in the zoo, the time had come when man in his native habitat figured as an exhibit. Camper was measuring facial angles, Blumenbach was making a comparative study of skulls, the Royal Society was so interested in the resemblance to man of the orang-outang that it meditated an expedition to Africa. Lords Kames and Monboddo pondered tails, teeth, and intestines as insignia of higher or lower degrees of rank in the chain of being. All this is fairly well known and is part of the winding path of the advancement of science. But the effect of these studies on philosophers and publicists gives their early stages peculiar interest. Herder, for example, was familiar with the work of almost every physiologist of note in the eighteenth century. Together with Linnaeus and Buffon and the narratives of travel, scientists like Haller, Swammerdam, Réaumur, Tyson, Camper, and Blumenbach are among the sources he cites most frequently. He refers with pride to his own inspection of skulls.

For Herder, as for Buffon, man is a natural-history subject. Indeed, since the history of man in all its ramifications, physical as well as psychic, is the theme of his *Ideen*, he is even more articulate on this topic. He is anxious to see established a "universal botanical geography for the history of man."[49] In assessing the influence of the *Ideen* one must never lose sight of this notion of Herder's that he can fit man into the universal scheme by viewing his history as he would that of a plant or tree. "The botanical science which groups plants according to the altitude and consistency of the soil, according to the conditions of the atmosphere, of water, and of temperature, is thus an obvious guide to a similar science in the kingdom of animals and men."[50] He adds in a note that Linnaeus' "*Philosophia botanica* is a classic model for several sciences" and wishes for a "*Philosophia anthropologica*" of the same kind. The study of the atmosphere, of mountains, rivers, plateaux, of new continents and of the routes of migration belongs as much to the history of the progression of the species Man, he says, as it does to the natural history of the earth. Even the history of civilization, which must compass man's struggle with other species for existence, is in large part zoological.

History, then, is Herder's Utopia as it is Vico's, and history for him is a cosmic performance, comprising not alone the civil and customary actions of men but the whole story of creation. The unifying theme in this gigantic pageant is that of the chain of being, stretching from the lowest to the highest powers, with man simply a link in the chain, and humanity, although itself the product of many labours, many sacrifices, and many sorrows, perhaps but a stage in the process of development. With this background in mind, it is easier to understand that Herder makes a great many statements which go counter to the general impressions one might receive from reading his work. By means of the great catch-all, the chain of being, he is able to reconcile an attitude of tolerance towards evil and destruction with a rather sentimental piety and fervent enthusiasm for humanity in the abstract. For the purpose of this discussion what matters is not the frame that Herder has given to his work, which is ill-adapted to the material it contains, but the impressions emanating from it.

To begin with, Herder insists that all human beings belong to the same great family and that they are all members of one species.[51] He indignantly pushes aside the suggestion that an inferior species of *genus homo* is to be found in the orang-outang or the *homme du bois*, and proclaims that men of different races are brothers:

> ... thou, O man, honour thyself: neither the pongo nor the gibbon is thy brother: the american and the negro are: these therefore thou shouldst not oppress, or murder, or steal; for they are men, like thee ....[52]

He is critical of the term "race" that over-zealous scientists have set up as a criterion of the differences among types of men; since these differences do not go very deep he considers that there is no need of such a term:

> In short, there are neither four or five races, nor exclusive varieties, on this Earth. Complexions run into each other: forms follow the genetic character: and upon the whole, all are at last but shades of the same great picture, extending through all ages, and over all parts of the earth.[53]

Even the notion of species evokes in Herder, as in Buffon, a kind of distrust, and he condemns indignantly the idea that the life of the individual could have no other value than its contribution to the existence of the species.[54]

Yet his valiant attempt to preserve a sense of the brotherhood of man was endangered by the very perspective he adopted. For, first, there is, in consequence of the biological approach, a heavy accent on variety without any adequate principle to reconcile the variable with the permanent aspects of man's nature.

> This plant has been created for the sea, that one for the swamp, this one loves the snow, the other the inundating rains of the tropical zone; and all these factors affect its form, its shape. Does not all this prepare us to expect the same varieties when we come to examine the organic structure of mankind, insofar as we are plants?[55]

As the same species of plant or animal may be seen to vary in different quarters of the globe, so man, too, appears in altered shape and guise to suit the exigencies of climate. The "locusts of the earth," the Kalmucks and the Mongols, are fitted to live in no country but their own steppes and mountains; the Arab "with his noble horse and tireless camel . . . is in perfect harmony with the desert."[56] The following passage brings out very clearly the connection of the idea of variability with the experience of comparisons based on travel:

> An European sheep acquires at the Cape of Good Hope a tail nineteen pounds in weight: in Iceland he puts out as many as five horns: in the county of Oxford, in England, he grows to the size of an ass: and in Turkey his

skin is variegated like a tiger's. Thus do all animals vary; and shall not man, who is also in the structure of his nerves and muscles an animal, change with the climate?[57]

In Books VI and VII of the *Ideen* Herder enters upon an extended discussion of the variations of man, and he concludes a chapter devoted to the subject of adaptation by saying that he could continue with comparisons from Kamschatka to Tierra del Fuego, for wherever men have settled they have taken root like trees and "produced foliage and fruit" appropriate to the climate.

Now it was easy, in the process of describing the appearance of man in different climates, to slip into the habit of suggesting the superiority of some and the inferiority of others. Thus, among the Chinese, Herder says, "Climate has merely reduced the broad face, little black eyes, stump nose, and thin beard [of the Mongols] to a softer, rounder form; and the taste of the Chinese seems to be as much a consequence of illconstructed organs, as despotism is of their form of government, and barbarism is of their philosophy."[58] The physiology of the Negro is an "oleaginous organization to sensual pleasure";[59] his skills and talents are limited accordingly, and at his unsuitability for the higher life of intellect he must not repine, for "Either no Africa should have been created, or it was requisite, that negroes should be made to inhabit Africa."[60]

If, therefore, Herder has stressed the unity and brotherhood of mankind, he has simultaneously abandoned the concepts that alone could give meaning to that unity. The conclusion that he draws from his study of the varieties of the human form is that "the greater part of man is of the animal kind: he has brought into the world only a capacity for humanity, which must first be formed in him by diligence and labour. In how few is it rightly formed! ... Throughout life the brute prevails over the man."[61] There is, then, no equality among men, except in those plastic elements that environment will shape into different creatures; and if there are not races in the usual sense of the word, there are peoples who are fated to be inferior, whose very function is to be miserable or brutish.[62] Respect must give way to pity as the cement that binds this unequal brotherhood.

There is no doubt that Herder's mind had been troubled by recent accounts of cannibalism in New Zealand as well as by the vivid descriptions he had read of the "poor wretches" of Tierra del Fuego. The more detailed accounts that were beginning to come back from the explorations in the Pacific called up not only the idyllic dream of life in Tahiti but evoked as well a dark picture of superstition and of man's inhumanity to man. Growing acquaintance with the "wild branches shot forth among the children of men" (so viel wilde Ranken . . . unter den Kinder der Erde aufgeschossen sind)[63] obviously brought painful reflections to Herder's mind. The effect of shock is revealed in one of the most striking passages of the *Ideen:*

> If man is proud of his reason, let him survey, across the stage of the world, the assemblage of his brothers, let him hearken to the dissonant sounds of their history. What inhuman barbarity is there to which a human being, a nation, even many nations, cannot become accustomed? Have not many peoples, perhaps even the majority, once eaten the flesh of their own kind? Is there any absurdity that imagination can now invent which was not at one time or another a belief sanctified by tradition? Therefore, man stands on as low a level as a rational creature can, for he is all his life not only a child in reason but is even in tutelage to the reason of others. Whatever influences play on him will shape him accordingly, and I am convinced that there is not, among the order of possible things, any human custom which some individual or some nation has not adopted. History exhausts the possible vices and virtues until in the end, here and there, a nobler form of human thought and virtue shines forth.[64]

It is the element of universality in the Law of Nature that is under attack; although Herder may say that he believes in the universal brotherhood of man, he obviously means it in quite a different sense. He exhorts the reader to understand that "the New Zealand cannibal and a Fenelon, a Newton and the wretched pesheray, are all creatures of one and the same species," only to exclaim a minute later that God alone knows "why he left on this his world both pesherays and new-zealanders."[65] It is indeed difficult for a man to embrace as his own kindred creatures whose mere existence is beyond his comprehension. In accordance with the principle of plenitude Herder consoles himself with the reflection that it was the *function* of these savages to be subhuman; "there is evidently a progressive scale from the man who borders on the brute to the purest genius in human form,"[66] *and both are equally necessary*. The application of the idea of the chain of being to the history of man goes directly contrary to the Law of Nature in its suggestion that it is necessary that some human beings should forever express the lower, some the higher, degrees of humanity. There is nothing in Herder's philosophy to deny that some men are *naturally* slaves; and although he would have abhorred the idea of a *Herrenvolk* in its modern form, there is no principle of his that would be a barrier to the notion of a people destined to rule and a people destined to serve. In the purely naturalistic conception of progress that he shares with his successors of modern Germany, there would be no theoretical reason why the peoples of Europe should not become the helots of a breed of self-styled supermen.

With nineteenth-century "organic" theories of the state in mind, we cannot but be struck by Herder's emphasis on the variation of groups rather than of individuals. In this he resembles Buffon, only for him it is the nation, not the species, in which collective existence is embodied. His nationalism stems from this source and from his interest in folk customs and in tradition. In the very passage in which he rejects the term race, arguing that it suggests differences among men which are not truly fundamental, he implies that national characteristics are more fundamental ("For every nation is one people, having its own national form, as well as its own language: the climate, it is true, stamps on each its mark ... but not sufficient to destroy the original character.")[67] It would probably be difficult for most students of political theory to realize that the following passage deals with a writer of the eighteenth century:

> The unit in the development of humanity is not the individual but the group. The individual by himself cannot achieve the fullest development and the most complete expression of his virtues and talents, he can only do this as an integral part of a group. . . . Moreover, the group which is the chief factor in the development of humanity is a group of a specific type; it is the national group or nationality. . . . [But] the development of the national individuality is also an end in itself, "for every nationality bears in itself the standard of its perfection, totally independent of all comparison with that of others."[68]

Yet this is the comment of a modern scholar on Herder. The author, Dr. Robert Ergang, sums up his study of Herder's nationalism in the statement, "To the individualism of the eighteenth century Herder opposed the collectivism of the nineteenth. . . . The great theme 'man' was no longer treated in such a way as to center on the individual, but on the national group. . . ."[69] About this aspect of Herder's thought there are two observations that must be made. One is that Herder's thoughts on nationalism abound in his favorite biological comparisons: he speaks of national organisms each "growing like a tree on its stem";[70] nations are plants, and like plants, they have a life-cycle of youth, maturity, and decay; "young" nations would, therefore, have more vitality than old ones. The other comment that deserves to be made here is that emphasis on the group was a natural outgrowth of comparisons based on the voyages. Under these circumstances, men were, after all, observed in groups; it was not the differences between individuals that mattered, but the difference between the whole lot of Tierra del Fuego people, or Tahitians, say, and their European visitors.[71] In addition, tribal life is perhaps more essentially a group life than any other (which is no doubt why in circumstances of extreme confusion or necessity tribal life even today has its advocates). The following passage will serve as an illustration of the connection in Herder's mind between tribalism and nationalism:

> The savage who loves himself, his wife and child with quiet joy and glows with limited activity for his tribe as for his own life is in my opinion a more real being than that cultivated shadow who is enraptured with the shadow of his whole species.... The former has room in his hut for every stranger.... The inundated heart of the idle cosmopolite is a home for no one.[72]

It is of some interest that this passage was quoted approvingly by Stein in his *Historischpolitische Betrachtungen*. It will not, perhaps, be found surprising that Herder regarded the German nation as a chosen people.[73] The nation or national group has taken on for him the confused connotations of "species"; he begins to think of the nation as a kind of transcendental entity, and when the nation or group is conceived of as a living thing, a *persona*, it easily becomes the object of superstition.

Herder's nationalism is but one aspect of the thoroughgoing relativism which permeates his philosophy. This relativism increases in effect, so to speak, as it narrows from the cosmic scheme of things to the scene of man's effort to govern himself by customs and moral standards, and, at last, by law.

The first level of relativism is that which defines man's place relative to the rest of creation. Herder's idea here, that man is a middle creature of a middle state, is familiar as a refrain of the Great Chain of Being. Placed above the animals but below the heavenly creatures, man's is an earthly intelligence, and his faculties are adapted to existence on this planet. More interesting is the idea that because man is in the midst of things and not outside creation he has no standard of comparison, and all his knowledge is thus infected with uncertainty: "We are not in the centre, but in the throng; like other worlds we float with the stream, and have no standard of comparison."[74]

The second phase of relativism is that in which man as a physical being varies in accordance with the physical environment in which he lives on the earth's surface; this has already been discussed as an aspect of the theme of variety. In most of the passages dealing with variations among men, Herder qualifies his statements so as to say: men vary as do plants, at least in those vegetative or organic powers they share with plants; or, man is in the structure of his muscles and nerves an animal, and must, therefore, vary in accordance with climate as animals do. But the implied reservation, that there are qualities in which men do not resemble plants and animals and do not vary, is not serious. For Herder regards the variations of man as a physical being, and the differences in the problems presented to him by his environment, as leading directly to differences in his ideas; and this constitutes the next level of relativism.

Thus reason itself, once thought of as the invariable and distinguishing characteristic of man, is partitioned out among the four quarters of the globe. Herder maintains that reason varies in accordance with the organic forces of man's being *(organische Kräfte, innere Kräfte)* and with the impressions he receives. As the vital powers act in conjunction with the climate, and as even the senses, though initially the same, similarly undergo changes in different modes of living, Herder argues that ideas must be confined by the region in which people live. The ideas of all indigenous peoples are so confined, "and when they declare that they understand certain words which express objects that are strange to them, we have a right thoroughly to doubt the truth of that assertion."[75] One of Herder's excursions into comparative mythology makes this point strongly:

> Compare the mythology of the Greenlanders with that of the Hindus, of the Lapps and the Japanese, of the Peruvians and the Negroes: it is a complete geography of the human imagination. If an Icelandic saga were read and expounded to a Brahmin, he would hardly be able to understand a single idea of it, any more than the Icelander would be able to understand the Vedas.[76]

It would not be difficult to concede this point, though it would not be to concede very much. And we may admire Herder's insight when he goes on to point out that the mythology of each people is the expression of the particular form in which nature appears to them. But Herder goes further. He sees in the relativity of customs a phenomenon that casts doubt on the possibility of men's sharing, through their common humanity, their most profound experiences:

> What one nation holds indispensable to the circle of its thoughts, has never entered into the mind of a second, and by a third has been deemed injurious. Thus we wander over the earth in a labyrinth of human fancies: but the question is; where is the central point of the labyrinth, to which all our wanderings may be traced, as refracted rays to the Sun.[77]

He falls back on the gloomy suggestion, again encouraging to tribalism, that nature has done all she can "not to extend our development but to circumscribe it, and to habituate us to the sphere where our life must develop."[78]

It is a small step from the belief that man's power to reason and his ideas vary with his environment, to the belief that law or custom lacks significance outside the time and place of its origin, and conversely, that even the most cruel laws or customs may be justified from the point of view of the peoples who have evolved them. This, which we may take as the fourth phase, is perhaps best described as moral relativism. Pursued far enough it renders any general moral judgment thoroughly impossible.

A curious confusion of ideas leads Herder to this position. He is, in fact, trying to show that peoples apparently the most barbarous have nevertheless some element of humanity. No Greek, no European, ever lived in as low a state as the New Zealander, he says, yet even the New Zealander has some feeling of humanity for those he recognizes as his brethren. He does not eat his own children. Likewise, the Eskimo's live burial of children or the Hottentot's slaying of the aged is the result of sad necessity, in our eyes an outrage of the laws of humanity, but no worse for the peoples whose custom it is than Western man's disregard of his own most sacred laws is for him. An argument of this kind demonstrates the lack of any general or transcendental idea of justice by which local customs may be measured. The fallacy in saying that the Aztecs were justified in their practice of human sacrifice because Cortez also was cruel should be apparent to anyone. Moreover, it does not follow from the fact that human sacrifice was a product of Aztec culture, that it was just even for the Aztecs. Herder confuses sympathy with people for what they may have been driven to do, or for what they know no better than to do, with tolerance of the evil itself. Thus cannibalism in his parlance becomes an example of the "law" of war:

> . . . their inhuman practice is a savage right of war *(ein grausames Kriegsrecht)*, to nourish their valour, and terrify their enemies. It is, therefore, nothing more or less, than the work of a gross political reason; which in those nations has overpowered humanity with regard to these few sacrifices to their country, as it is overpowered by us europeans, even in the present day, in some other respects.[79]

Herder expends a great deal of effort in this manner, trying to bring the lives and customs of remote peoples within the orbit of humanity. Looked at from their own point of view, the savages show, relatively speaking, if not as high a type of humanity, at least as *much* humanity, as much loyalty to their laws and customs, as the European. For the concept of universal reason he struggles to substitute one of universal humanity, but "humanity" seems to mean simply obedience to prevailing local customs.

One must sympathize with Herder's desire to comprehend the lives of strange peoples still in a primitive stage of culture, and with his realization that the customs of these people must be looked at from their point of view before they can be understood at all. So far, so good; but there is nothing in this experience of comparisons to indicate that all moral judgments must be purely relative. Still moving along the same track Herder declares that judgments of the superiority of one way of life over another must be put aside:

> Thus the difference between enlightened and unenlightened, cultivated and uncultivated nations, is not specific; it is only in degree. This part of the picture of nations has infinite shades, changing with place and time: and, like other pictures, much depends upon the point of view from which we examine it.[80]

European culture, then, becomes but one among many others:

> If we take the idea of european cultivation for our standard, this is to be found only in Europe: and if we establish arbitrary distinctions between cultivation and enlightening of the mind, neither of which, if it be genuine, can exist independently of the other, we are losing ourself still more in the clouds.[81]

So the natural-history point of view is on its way to dominate the study of ethics, politics, and law as well as the evolution of physical beings. Herder's purpose was, of course, to show that there is a place for every people and to rebuke a parochialism content with the attitude that in the life of the so-called backward people there is nothing superior, nothing worth while. His intention was really humanitarian; he wished to defend primitive people against the arrogance and domination of the Europeans. The danger of his uncritical relativism is not in what it includes but in what it omits. If cannibalism can be gently explained as a "right of war" to the people who practice it, and is therefore not to be condemned as absolutely inhuman, what is to make us withhold our sympathy from a tribe of cannibals who may be powerful enough to eat everybody else? It does not matter that Herder would have been astonished and dismayed if such an event were to come to pass, or that he would have had a strong feeling of disapproval and repugnance towards it. The significant point is that without some such conception as that of a higher law, a Law of Nature, or universal ideal of justice, there is nothing in his or any man's philosophy to say why we should not sympathize with conquest and aggrandizement. And if the only sense of law is in the bosom of each tribe or nationality, force alone can be the arbiter of their disputes.

It remains to describe Herder's tendency towards anti-rationalism. Following Buffon's sketch of the growth of human intelligence, in his "De l'Homme," and Rousseau's dramatization of similar ideas in *Emile*, Herder describes reason as a capacity that is not innate, but which must be developed. This is a point of view with which we are now perfectly familiar. Exploration of the connection between reason and experience should have been an improvement over the somewhat shallow rationalism of the eighteenth century. Herder's thinking on this subject, however, slants towards an obscurantism that foreshadows the most destructive form of anti-rationalism. The substitution of belief in instinct, will, and unconscious forces for belief in the efficacy of reason is a characteristic feature of what Professor Hans Kohn has justly called the *Verzauberung* of the nineteenth century.[82]

Herder begins simply enough with the idea that reason is not an automatic mechanism that man is born with, but something that is acquired through practice and experience. In the long period of dependence and of learning through which young human beings, in this unlike animals, must pass, the influence of other people is of immense importance. The child is not yet fully human, the human being is the *sum* of a process of development. This is what we should call, I suppose, a genetic theory. But what is reason, once attained? Here is where Herder's tendency towards anti-rationalism appears. First, reason depends greatly on tradition:

> Reason is an aggregate of the experiences and observations of the mind, the end result of the education of man, which the pupil finally achieves for himself, working from others' models, like an artist in a foreign land.
> Therein lies the distinctive character of human beings . . . that we achieve humanity only through lifelong practice . . . from that fact it follows that human history is necessarily a whole, that it is a chain of sociability and formative tradition from the first to the last link.[83]

In this manner reason, first shown to be dependent upon experience, melts into tradition—a force to which in many circumstances it might be thought to be diametrically opposed. And Herder himself conceives this dependence of man upon others and this borrowing from the past as a mark of weakness, evidence of the fact that men are not born human, but only become so gradually. Last, in the remarkable passage already quoted, Herder winds up to a peroration in which he exhorts the man proud of his reason to hearken to the "dissonant sounds" of his savage brothers and concludes with an apostrophe to tradition as the great chain of social being that compensates for reason's weakness. The passage is typical of the confusion of Herder's thought. Whatsoever things are good he admires: freedom, intelligence, generosity. But when these are resigned to the anonymous stewardship of tradition, when tradition is said to preserve and hand on the follies and mistakes of the past as well as its accomplishments, and when this bulging portmanteau, this "fardel of old stories," is said to be the voice of God, we are left helpless to choose between good and evil, and our actions can have no principle but a hapless inspiration which may lead us we know not where. I think it is not too much to say that in Herder's *Ideen* the change from the universal ideal of reason to acceptance of the universal dominance of irrational forces has already begun. First, the idea of reason as Inner Light or as Common Sense is abandoned in favour of a genetic account of its development. Then, the development of reason is shown not to depend upon the individual's experience alone or upon that of his contemporaries, but upon vague "formative" traditions from the past. The equation, Law of Nature = Reason, has been transformed into Law of Nature = Custom or Tradition.

It will not escape the reader's notice that Herder limits the meaning of reason in identifying it with some kind of analytical faculty or power to deal with abstract ideas. Reason in this sense, he argues, is not a universal possession of man. He then substitutes for it, as the only kind of thought that all savage nations possess, this vague feeling of awe towards the "unseen powers." Proof of this feeling he finds in the widespread belief in immortality which is demonstrated by customs of the burial of the dead. Instinctive belief in survival after death is the one thing that distinguishes the dying man from an animal; ". . . man in dying is distinguished from the brute by this general article of belief alone."[84]

In short, Herder has dissolved the concept of reason by

presenting it as a combination of the action of "vital powers" and of "formative traditions," and by maintaining in addition that the universal mark of man is not reason but a vague religious instinct—a religious instinct which does not, cannot, make any distinction between reverence towards the highest that is known and sheer idolatry or Moloch rites of sacrifice. And observe the process by which Herder has arrived at these conclusions: the criterion of what is universal is what may be discovered to prevail among primitive societies, for that, so to speak, must be the lowest common denominator of humanity. Tribal traditions and myths are not, he thinks, the invention but the inheritance of early peoples. Yet myths were originally devised to account for actual facts. It would seem, then, that the power to reason from experience was the full prerogative only of the first men, and all the thought of their descendants must be merely declarative of the experience of their ancestors. Not that this conclusion would not have seemed as absurd to Herder as it does to us, especially in view of his deep belief in progress and development. But there is in philosophies like his no discussion of the function of reason in discovery, or of the way in which growth takes place through criticism when the developed faculty of reason recognizes some of the "formative traditions" as childish or unjust. And it is curious that Herder, although aware of the cruelties, superstitions, and deceits which have marked the path of religious tradition as conserved by a privileged caste, can find no principle in his religious instinct by which the falsehoods of the credulous or the persecutions of the powerful can be distinguished from beliefs more worthy of man's intelligence. In this uncritical choice of religious instinct working through tradition as the criterion of humanity, there is implicit a strengthening all at once of tribalism, of anti-rationalism, and of relativism. We may admire in Herder as in Vico his studious interest in the material for study to be found in the life of primitive tribes, as well as his unfeigned sympathy for the "poor wretches" he so eloquently describes and his determination to understand them as human beings. All this represents a real advance over the complacent contentment with European civilization that was characteristic of some Enlightenment thinkers and is still the creed of hundred-percenters wherever they are found today. But in trying to make this fuller, amended picture of a State of Nature once more the basis of a set of general ideals, Herder substituted poorer standards for the ones which he considered too advanced to represent primitive man in the human family.

In abandoning reason as the universal criterion of human nature, Herder, like Vico, had also abandoned the objective. There is, in fact, no reason why the primitive, whether as idealized by poets or as described by scientists, should be taken as the measure of humanity. Nor is there any reason why tradition should be given any special value as tradition, unless men, by their own unclouded judgment or mature decision, should approve its content or the way of life built on it as still good for them. There are good traditions and bad traditions, and even good traditions should be accepted through a free act of respect rather than through fear or superstitious awe. Inasmuch as the freedom won by the Renaissance and the Reformation was gained in large part only by the most determined struggle, intellectually and politically, against the authority of the past, this rediscovery of authority in the form of tradition must be regarded as another aspect of the "second Counter-Reformation."

Many years after Herder, Nietzsche summed up in a few aphorisms the essence of the intellectual counter-movement which in our time, by force of arms, threatened to enslave the world. "The principal innovation . . . instead of moral values nothing but naturalistic values. Naturalization of morality. In the place of sociology a doctrine of the forms of domination."[85] The point that I wish to bring out as strongly as possible is that a tendency toward the substitution of "naturalistic values" for moral values can be observed as early as the eighteenth century, and that it is in part the result of laying aside the theory of the Law of Nature, with its emphasis on reason and the universal meaning of justice, for a crudely considered philosophy of value based on a blending of popular biology and history. It has already been remarked that Buffon sensed an implicit change of values in the application to human affairs of the point of view of natural history. In Herder this recognition is more explicit.

The belief that evil and destruction are a necessary part of progress is not novel, but it is interesting to find it in Herder springing from a combination of biological and historical notions. His natural history studies suggest to him that the appearance of higher species is preceded and prepared for by the destruction of many others; man, therefore, cannot hope to be exempt from the working of destructive forces in his own history: "In a system of changeable things, if there be progress, there must be destruction: apparent destruction, that is; or a change of figures and forms."[86] Similarly, in political history, war and desolation serve as a brilliant contrast to more peaceful times, and indeed, may be considered a necessary stimulant: "Only amid storms can the noble plant flourish . . . the seed germinates more beautifully in a subsequent period from the ashes of the good, and when irrigated with blood seldom fails to shoot up to an unfading flower."[87] It is typical that in the passage just quoted Herder resorts to a comparison with plant life to bring out his point about the history of man. From the point of view of the naturalist, man-made standards are not important; in the eyes of a superior being men may have no more value than a tree.[88] In another illustration (which he employs, as a matter of fact, to urge impartiality on the historian) the familiar theme of the principle of plenitude is brought together with a reference to the comparative method of the naturalist:

The naturalist who seeks to find out and classify all the species of the natural kingdom has no preference for either rose or thistle, skunk and sloth and elephant have an equal value.... Nature indeed ... has allowed to germinate all that time, place and living force could bring forth. All that can be, is; all that can develop, does, if not today, then tomorrow.[89]

Or, in the countryman's proverb remembered by George Eliot from her childhood, "There must be some such to be some of all sorts."

From the naturalistic background, then, comes the attitude of indifference, while historicism contributes the conservative principle. For, applied to history, the principle of plenitude tells each man to stay in his place—the familiar creed of "my station and its duties": "What and wherever thou wast born, O man, there thou art, and there thou shouldst be: quit not the chain, set not thyself above it, but adhere to it firmly."[90] In terms reminiscent of Vico, Herder finds it a "law" of history that the tyrant deserves to conquer and that the slave was born to be a slave. "We may take it as a general law of history that no people will be oppressed except those that wish to be oppressed and therefore deserve to be slaves. Only the coward is born a servant; the stupid man is destined by nature to serve the clever. Therefore each is well enough off in his position and would be unhappy if he had to give orders."[91] A passage that today requires no comment.

With typical inconsistency Herder goes on to say that the slave in chains can be free, while despots are often the most unhappy slaves. It is not that Herder himself admired despots or tyrants, or wished to promote slavery—we know, for example, with what enthusiasm he welcomed the French Revolution. But many a man has been a friend of liberty who had little or no understanding of the principles required for its maintenance. No matter what the personal opinions of the author, a historical fatalism like Herder's is inevitably reactionary; it must be content not only to submit to opportunism or violence, but even to praise it, when successful, as the expression of natural forces working through the strongest.

Applying to history the notions of struggle and growth he had absorbed from biology, and combining with them the curious fatalism of the principle of plenitude as understood by the eighteenth century, Herder left all questions of justice to be settled by the survival of the fittest. Long before Darwin the idea of the survival of the fittest had soaked into political thought. From this admittedly incomplete analysis of some of the ideas of Vico, of Buffon, and of Herder, we have separated out certain key concepts: the concept of struggle as being of itself beneficial, the concept of variability beginning to take the place of belief in the unity of mankind, the concept of the importance of group or whole over against that of the individual, the concept of tradition or custom or unanalyzable feeling as being, rather than reason, the characteristic mark of man. The foundation has been laid for the relativism of the nineteenth century, in which ideas are regarded only as weapons in the life struggle of a biologic group.

At the end of the eighteenth century, then—the age of belief in the unity of mankind, in the universality of justice, in reason and in liberty—ideas of a directly contrary nature have already been expressed by influential writers. The reason why these ideas became popular and the reason why they were uncritically accepted, at least in Germany, as premises of political theory, is a problem of great interest in the morphology of fascism. It is not that the presence of these ideas "in the air" accounted for the building of the Prussian tradition or for the eventual succession of its present-day offspring, Nazism. The reaction against the French Revolution in one century, the reaction against Versailles in another, economic stress and strain, industrial and population changes, are well recognized as among the moving forces in both periods. I believe, however, that what men think good, what they will expend effort to attain, in short, their ideals, powerfully affect their behaviour. If the key notions of historicism and of the organic philosophy had not been available, if they had not continued to appeal to minds like those of Nietzsche and Treitschke and Hitler, the subsequent history of Germany could hardly have been the same. Her energy must have been driven into other channels. And because I do not think that in intellectual history more than elsewhere, whatever has been, must have been, and that all that can be, is, I shall pass on to some evaluation of these key concepts in comparison with those of the Law of Nature which they supplanted for a time.

IV. THE SCOPE OF JUSTICE

> . . . the spirit of Nationality may be defined (negatively but not inaccurately) as a spirit which makes people feel and act about a part of any given society as though it were the whole of that society.—Arnold J. Toynbee, *A Study of History*, I, 9.

WE SHOULD NOT EXPECT the terms natural law or Law of Nature to find currency again. An irreversible change in thought has taken place; at very least, it has indicated that the cluster of concepts designated by the phrase, "Law of Nature," is, in the form upon which that phrase sets its stamp of approval, the product of a premature readiness to accept as understood ideas that we have yet to fathom. Through the labours of investigators following upon the track of Vico, of Buffon, and of Herder we have been made aware of the diversity of things, of the interaction between human beings and the conditions in which they live, and of the degree to which nearly all social norms reflect the process of adaptation.

Yet adaptation has a purpose; the purpose is life; and life persists in meaning more than mere survival. We need not, in our sophistication, go so far as Hume—if indeed it is sophistication—to declare that "the word natural is commonly taken in so many senses, and is of so loose a significance, that it seems vain to dispute whether justice be natural or not."[1] On the contrary, we are compelled in each generation to ask, in questions of different form but with the same intent, whether or not there is in our constitution as people some basic need for justice, and whether that need may be understood as from man to man, person to person, in spite of human differences.

That, essentially, is the problem offered by the study of the Law of Nature, and the answer of that school of thought has been in the affirmative. Stripping the term "nature" of all the mysteries and ambiguities that have grown up around it, we shall find that it indicates a belief that justice is independent of local conditions: not that, in practice, or in the law courts, justice can be administered without reference to the concrete situation, but that beyond the concrete situation there is a bond between man and man, a knowledge of good, the meaning of which can never be exhausted by the local, the changing, the temporary. Justice involves a continuous objective reference.

The essence of the Law of Nature is further, a belief in justice as logically prior to the establishment of any state and to the ordinances of positive law; and we should add, ethically superior as well as logically prior, since it is not merely a formal quality that has to be described. Logical priority and ethical superiority neither mean nor imply historical priority. It may be conceded that the concept of justice does not and perhaps cannot appear earlier than life in a community and that it is in some sense a product of social experience, although that does not exhaust its meaning. But even if the appearance of a concept of justice were shown to have occurred very late in the evolution of human society, that would neither detract from its genuineness nor reduce its power.

Nor does it matter in this connection that "rights," from the point of view of the lawyer or of the historian, are the creation of law; for it remains true, as Professor Morris Cohen has so clearly stated, that "while laws and government protection create legal rights, the effectiveness of this protection depends upon the recognition of previously existing fundamental psychic or social interests. To the extent that these interests exist and demand protection even prior to the specific law which meets their demand, they are the raw material of natural rights ... interests and claims do exist prior to and not as creatures of those laws which they call into being."[2] To speak of fundamental psychic or social interests, of claims and demands, is to speak of human nature in a manner acceptable to the modern reader.

Let us be clear, also, that the concept of the Law of Nature is intrinsically of superior ethical value to the authority wielded by any institution which may be devised to further the realization of moral purpose, such as a church. For this reason the Law of Nature as it appears in ecclesiastical theory is usually confused or contradictory. Obviously, no exclusive right of interpretation of this concept can belong to any agency, ecclesiastical or otherwise; such institutions are to be judged by the Law of Nature, not to be its judges.

Finally, it should be understood beyond doubt that the essential contribution of the Law of Nature is to the theory of government, and not to the practice of law. It indicates certain moral constants which, if we find them to be real in our own experience, should govern the relations of man to man. It is a guiding concept for the theory of government because it tells us of a quality of behaviour that will hold for all people in the absence of direct personal relationships. When we try to frame specific instruments for the ordering of social relations in any specific age or place for any one portion of society, we should never lose sight of these moral constants. But there is much more that we must be conscious of, and much more—in the way of custom and tradition and the strength of institutions—by which we shall inevitably be influenced. No one authoritative set of deductions can be made from the main elements of the Law of Nature. No one set of rules can be valid for all the situations, old and new, known and unknown, that have to be dealt with in the law courts. It is not the function of the Law of Nature to take the place of social evolution. We must be clear whether we intend by the Law of Nature a set of standards for the attainment of justice (and the phenomena of novelty and variability do not remove the need for these standards) or a concrete body of laws deducible from the standards, which can in fact represent justice to every one under all circumstances. To state the alternative is at once to solve the problem. Certainly the latter of the two, a universally valid declarative body of law, is impossible. No general principles act of themselves. They are present to guide and inform choice; but they do not determine the nature of the material to be chosen nor the specific mould in which it is to be shaped.

The concept of the Law of Nature has outlived its usefulness in jurisprudence. The illusion that the Law of Nature tells us what justice is, rather than what it ought to be, led to its being displaced. Displaced, not abandoned: for even the most subtle advocates of law as "social engineering" have not left the ideals of reasonableness behind.[3] If we can see the Law of Nature as being, fundamentally, an ideal of justice in government rather than a divinely dispensed, mathematically deduced code, the displacement can appear as a creative change in thought. Freely conceived, the Law of Nature is a description of the purpose outside the law for which the law exists, and it is a measure of the moral aim of social action, respect for which can alone entitle any government to the willing allegiance of its citizens.

The beginning of the creative change took place in the eighteenth century, the time of the natural law's greatest practical effect as well as the time of its obsolescence in theory. As we have said, it was from the description of the general character of the Law of Nature, not its supposed content, that eighteenth century ideas of right were derived. The political writers realized that it was a set of standards for the making of law by men, not the law itself that men would make. If the Law of Nature had been clearly understood as a set of standards for the use and interpretation of law, as well as for the plain making of it in legislation, the words of the historical school would have been largely wasted.

If the doctrine of the Law of Nature was fundamentally an aspect of political theory which tremendously influenced the development of law, the "historical" school of jurisprudence was an offshoot of legal research that has in its turn affected political theory: more by the omissions it encourages than by the positive ideas it contributes. In such fashion the beginning—but not the fullness—of self-knowledge is often destructive as well as temporarily stimulating.

The work of historicism (we have seen the tendency in Vico and in Herder) was to discard the idea of a universal law. The more expert investigators who followed them showed that it would be impossible, even if it were desirable, to deduce from general propositions the specific laws that should govern men of different habits and customs, living in different stages of development. It was shown that law had evolved in close association with other aspects of social life, and that this was always likely to be so. It was further shown that there was a considerable difference among the peoples as to what constitutes good behaviour and as to what measures should be adopted to encourage the acceptance of social norms by the members of a group.

This was the direction of the line of research laid down by the historical school—with its development in detail we are not concerned. As in so many other cases where new knowledge has affected the course of men's thinking, it is difficult to find any clear discussion of principle accompanying the gathering of facts. For, to begin with, have we any reason to believe that the assumptions of the historical school rendered sufficiently intelligible the facts collected by its labours, or that the empirical data gathered did actually refute the main elements of the Law of Nature theory? The value or usefulness of any investigation, scientific or historical, must not blind us to the faulty principles in accordance with which the data is often arranged. It is, as a matter of fact, very often such general principles which exert most influence over the public mind, although they may receive least attention from the investigators themselves. It should be observed, too, in conjunction with the sway of the historical school and of the relativistic doctrines still so influential in social thought, that when a new method —for example that of history or sociology—comes into use, there is a tendency to set up the principles of the method as an absolute in place of those absolutes which the new study has displaced. To the operation of this tendency, I think, we may attribute the importance of "instrumental" ideas in recent social, legal, and political thought. That is to say, phenomena of adaptation were being observed, so it was natural to find in adaptation a principle as well as a fact. This tendency was strengthened by the simultaneous development of "natural history"; in Darwin, for example, we find a meeting ground of the ideas derived from biology and from historical studies of a different type; the result was to make the process of history, of change, of adaptation, seem to be an almost cosmic scheme.

In such fashion, then, "history" instead of "nature" was set up as a criterion; but in spite of its claim to greater realism it was no less an a priori concept than the one that it displaced. Critics of the so-called historical school in jurisprudence have remarked on this. Professor Cohen, for one, finds the historicism of the nineteenth century "in some respects more mischievous than the rationalism of the eighteenth. In the writings of Hegel, Karl Marx, and of the German historical school of jurisprudence, the real nature of historicism as an inverted or romantic form of rationalism becomes apparent."[4] Concepts such as Hegel's absolute, Marx's system of production, and the historian's *Volksgeist* "function in an entirely *a priori*, rationalistic way."[5] Professor Pound, from another point of view, has shown that the historical school of jurisprudence, in particular, had no adequate sense of the relationship of historical knowledge to the framework of the law. Savigny, he remarks, "assumed the seventeenth- and eighteenth-century doctrine that law was only declaratory, and simply put a historical foundation under it in place of its original philosophical foundation."[6] Also, the selection of periods for study revealed special interests and predispositions and was out of touch with actual legal materials. "After a century of historical jurisprudence along these lines we have come to think that it was not a historical school at all."[7] When history is taken as a principle of behaviour, it no less than "nature" has within itself an "ought-to-be," an admiration perhaps for a given set of institutions or a desire to maintain the status quo. The danger is that the "ought-to-be" is concealed; it is withdrawn from the judgment of the forum, and perhaps given into the custody of some social priesthood sympathetic to the group that happens to be in power.

These unfavourable judgments reflect upon the founders of historicism no less than on their heirs. For there is a remarkable continuity in the main assumptions guiding the school. Is it Herder or is it Goering who says that "the eternal right, the moral right, . . . grows from father to son and is therefore born of the blood of a people. Therefore the race and blood related peoples have their laws and understand them. You would hardly find people in the South Seas who would understand nordic-germanic justice. What is justice to them and understood by them as such, is incomprehensible to us and is frowned upon."[8] Actually, it is Goering, speaking to the German Academy of Justice in 1934, but it might as well have been Herder, writing the

Ideen in 1784. Treitschke, himself a thinker in the main line of inheritance, emphasized Herder's contribution to the supplanting of the Law of Nature theory by historicism, and the consequent overthrow of belief in universal justice. The Law of Nature, Treitschke said, "was first scientifically overthrown in Germany in the seventeenth and eighteenth [*sic*] centuries after Herder had pitted himself against it. Herder was unsurpassed as a stimulator of thought, and his ideas were taken up, shaped, and worked out by others. The way was opened for the historical science of law of Eichhorn, Niebuhr, and Savigny. By them law was treated as a living thing, developing with the nation."[9] The presence of this continuity is, indeed, the chief reason for examining the sources of historicism and the ideas allied with it instead of tracing its later development, for in the work of the earlier writers the grain of the guiding assumptions is not yet overlaid with masses of material.

History as a mode of investigation which yields accurate facts about the past has a value of its own; it is, further, of the greatest use in informing us of relationships of contiguity in time and of patterns of survival, change or development. In rejecting the a priori notion of "History" as a social norm we are not reflecting on the validity of historical study; we simply assert that neither the method nor the material content of historical study can be considered a principle of value—and yet that is what the proponents of historicism have taken it to be.[10] "History" is clearly inferior even to the vague term "Nature" as a social norm. The fact that a given institution develops in accordance with historical conditions does not mean that another kind of institution would not have been better, nor does it necessarily mean that another kind of institution would not have been possible. Historicism always bore tyranny concealed within it. "It is not for you, Everyman," it says, "to judge what the law should be; it is for us who have the right to interpret history to say what it is to be." If we were to follow the criterion of historicism, of tradition, of adaptation all the way—leaving aside, as in practice we cannot afford to do, any intention to deceive us on the part of interested groups—we should be left with an ethics of strategy alone; and universal strategy is no less than universal anarchy or nihilism. If the norm of "History" is compared with the first of the main elements of the Law of Nature, then the idea that Hume made light of, the idea that justice is natural, must as a principle of political reflection be judged superior to the notion that law is at best merely "a living thing developing with the nation." Though it is quite obvious that law does develop with the life of the nation or political unit, that life has some quality, some aim —it is that we must judge, and that which, under the most diverse conditions, has become sufficiently conscious to make judgment possible.

To put the problem by means of an example: laws such as the Nuremberg laws of Germany must either be approved as a development of the life of the nation and therefore good, because in accordance with history (which is no more than to say that they happened), or we must say, with the founders of the Law of Nature, that whether or not such laws are a product of the nation's development, their justice or injustice must be shown on other grounds. It will make little difference if we consider laws to be purely the product of social demand, rather than the product of history: it is quite possible that from time to time groups of people will demand benefits for themselves at the expense of others, and even that they will demand punitive measures against innocent people, merely to satisfy their prejudice or superstition. That such incidents *will* take place and *have* taken place can never mean that they *should* take place. Nor can it mean, as it sometimes has to weary scholars, that the judgment, "they should not have taken place," is an empty one. It is in that way that the influence of historicism is still widespread: in the embarrassment which today inhibits so many people with a little learning from affirming their hope for mankind in any downright and hearty form.

There is, notwithstanding, a core of strength in the historical school, which partly explains its wide effect. It lies in the claims, the necessities, and the obstacles that are represented by the unhappy word, self-determination. It is not a view that can ever be disposed of, even if it can be shown to be inferior or incomplete; on its own level it can stand for felt needs and values that must be taken into account in any more general resolution of equalities and inequalities. We must reckon with the fact that people will always start for any destination with the impetus of what they want. To change their goal, we must affect what they want; but that can never be a successful change unless we are willing to understand what they begin by wanting. That is not too hard if we will go down to the primitive level on which people are not unlike, and, recognizing their version of all the basic needs we know, build from that.

It must be called to the attention of historicists, past and present, that the very disparities which they see as insurmountable gaps among people could never be observed were it not for the chance of comparison. The point of view from which comparisons are made must always be general; and observation of differences is a long step towards the discovery of common elements of life, both of the more simple and the more transcendent kind. Herder, for example, points out that the myths of the Greenland Eskimo are unintelligible to the Hindu; but he neglects the fact that he, the man of general culture, is able to compare them.[11] The traveller who observes these amazing insularities has been to Greenland, say, and to India, either in actual experience or in his putting together of the accounts of others. It is more than probable that today there are Hindus who have expert knowledge of the myths of other people, doubtless including the Eskimos. But it still seems to take almost an effort of will to imagine the possibility that peoples who cannot now understand each other because they have no common experience, may at some later point be able to reach a more general state of knowledge in which, to be sure, each will live his own life and not the life of the other, but each will take the life of the other into his ken. It is no accident but an admirable symmetry of things that this exchange of understanding, this transcendence of self-knowledge, is the result of relationships of kindness and friendliness rather than of enmity. The savage tribesman will grow to know and partly to understand the stranger who behaves peacefully towards him, sooner than the man who comes to kill and to destroy. Justice, or self-transcendence through an acknowledgment of value for the other, is an ideal only because it is first a fact; the possibility of this conception grows out of the act which gives it being.

A simple and amusing example of the recognition that justice is a self-transcending virtue may be given from an incident that is related in Anson's Voyages. Anson, in the course of his adventures off the coast of South America, had taken as a prize a ship named the *Santa Teresa de Jesus*. She had ten Spanish passengers on board, three of them women. These people had been led to expect barbarous treatment at the hands of the English and were frightened and apprehensive of the cruelties they thought they would receive. But, contrary to their fears, all of them were treated with kindness and civility, and what seemed to astonish them most, not only were the women left unmolested, but special care was taken for their comfort and safety. When at last the prisoners were put ashore at a Spanish town they were all enthusiastic in their praise of the commander:

> A Jesuit in particular, whom the commodore had taken, and who was an ecclesiastick of some distinction, could not help expressing himself with great thankfulness for the civilities he and his countrymen had found on

board . . . ; adding that his usage of the men prisoners was such as could never be forgot . . . but that his behaviour to the women was so extraordinary, and so extremely honourable, that he doubted all the regard due to his own ecclesiastical character would be scarcely sufficient to render it credible. Indeed we were afterwards informed that he and the rest of our prisoners had not been silent on this head, . . . the Jesuit in particular, as we were told, having on [Anson's] account interpreted in a lax and hypothetical sense that article of his church which asserts the impossibility of hereticks being saved.[12]

Here, in this revision of the concept of heaven so as to include just men who would be excluded by strict adherence to tradition, there is a more striking example of the movement from value to one's self to value for others than had been manifested in Anson's own simpler and really more common form of self-transcending behaviour.

To balance the idea that the process of comparison or the observation of difference points the way to the very standards it is sometimes taken to deny, let us put the fact that general ideals such as justice are frequently used as a cloak for self-interest. It frequently happens that the traditional way of settling a problem, the way that is claimed to be just, operates to the advantage of one party and to the detriment of another. When a group receives an injury or suffers defeat at the hands of another group whose cause is identified with universal ideals, the injured or defeated group may as a kind of intellectual revenge reject the ideals themselves. Instead of saying, "The ideal of justice (or equality, or what you will) is not at work here," the group that conceives itself to be injured may assert that the ideal itself of justice is insincere, hollow, hypocritical, decadent.[13] A recoil from the universal takes place because the universal is identified with the cause of a particular nation. We have seen this phenomenon in the contact of Western civilization with that of the East, or of the French ideals of the Enlightenment with the Germany of the Napoleonic wars. The group or nation undergoing such a violent intellectual reaction may set up its own traditions and interests as the sole norm or ideal, and thus indulge in an intense isolationism or tribalism.

Once such an intellectual reaction has set in, and the bonds of community with mankind are broken, there are likely to be demands which do not grow out of any injustice and are not excused by defeat, but express only a thirst for power and domination. But such a conflict between considerable groups of men, even if the right is clearly on one side, is an indication that the society or common locus of action in which both exist has become too narrow, has ceased to grow. It is either too exclusive to allow for an adjustment of mutual needs or too disunited to give effect to its ideals. Thus a flat denial by one party or nation of all sense in the general concept of justice held by the others usually calls for a drastic revision of the forms and institutions in which that concept has been expressed; and this is true, even though such a revision will not and should not give to the insurgent party its original demand. It is, accordingly, in the nature of justice that its meaning can never be exhausted by any given state of affairs; it does not change, but it is never complete; it contains in itself the possibility of revision and growth. And the spring of that possibility, the source of that growth, may lie in the occasions or circumstances which have given encouragement to what seems a rival theory: historicism, or historical relativism used as an expression of self-assertion. Further, it is to be observed that the general concept of justice, or as it was called, the Law of Nature, is connected with the idea of a greater society to which all belong; when there is a conflict between belief in justice and the ideas of a Carneades or a German minister of justice, one may guess—the topic is not to be explored here—that it is part of a movement of disintegration of a great society or of the formation of a greater society.

It follows that the historical criterion is not to be rejected but is to be considered entirely subordinate to the general concept of justice. Representing what any portion of people have long thought just for themselves, or what they refuse to accept as just in a prevailing situation, it brings us information not to modify the ideal of universal justice, but to extend its range of actualization and to make its operation more subtle and delicate. The problem of the contrast between historicism and the general concept of justice is in large the same as, in detail, the problem offered by the place within the Law of Nature of the element of variability.

It was the especial interest of some nineteenth-century writers taking part in the "revival" of natural law to make a place within the Law of Nature for the phenomenon of variability.[14] Not only the thinking of the historical school proper, but the influence of later research in sociology and anthropology was being felt. But the influence of the historical school on some of these writers—notably upon the neo-Kantians—was to result in an impoverishment of structural concepts and a resort to the position that the principles of just law must be purely formal and can have no experiential content. It is worth looking at this development in the work of two writers, Giorgio del Vecchio and Rudolf Stammler, who may be taken as its most interesting representatives.

History is for del Vecchio the starting point of any consideration of law, and history discloses a great variety of legal concepts and institutions. "Every historical system," he says, "determines in its own way what law is and what law is not; the same act or relation may be differently qualified in different ages or by different peoples".[15] But del Vecchio sees, as did the older writers, that it is systems of positive law which vary, while the general concept of justice is altogether of a different order. He does not fall into the confusion of thinking that variations in positive law or legal institutions make impossible the conceiving of any general standards of justice beyond these changes. Although he perceives the errors and omissions in past systems of natural law, he holds that the arguments used against it are wide of the mark; they are mainly based on the affirmation that law is only positive, "a simple affirmation which has not been and cannot be proved, but is believed out of respect to the dogma of a passing philosophy."[16] And so he finds that arguments based on this hypothesis are reducible to the proof that natural law does not exist as positive law, which is a begging of the question. The teaching of the natural law, he says, contains "all the characteristics of a psychological necessity, which is not disproved, but confirmed, by the number of ways in which the concept itself is reached and by the number of demonstrations given of it."[17]

There is certainly some inconsistency in del Vecchio's own approach to the concept of natural law. On the one hand, in Platonic strain, he thinks of it as "a system of the highest truths, not sensible but rational, and . . . independent of the existence of common institutions in all nations, and apparent disagreements with reality."[18] On the other hand, he finds strong confirmation of natural law standards in comparative jurisprudence and ethnological research.

> The modern studies, by whose light the variety in the forms of life and the difference according to time and place of both men and nations are more clearly seen, have shown with equal clearness that there are deep-rooted similitudes and continuous analogies, and even true and actual equalities of principle and institutions, among various peoples in different ages. We can proclaim with certainty that what Cicero called the "insignis humani generis similitudo" is always clearly shown by the customs and laws of all races. Now, after the latterday studies, based on biological ideas of conduct, there is less justification than ever for holding that life has not fixed conditions determined by its essential functions, which necessarily result in uniform elements of activity and thought in every individual and society.[19]

Likewise, he finds that the history of law shows a progressive recognition of the equality of man, and that "not as a mere ethical demand or metaphysical postulate" but as living reality, shown by the fact that personal protection, originally reserved to members of the tribal group and denied to strangers, "has been gradually extended to a larger circle, until for certain purposes it includes all mankind."[20]

For del Vecchio as for Grotius, natural law and international law find common ground. " 'The national character' of law, the slogan of the historical school, is a sign of incomplete development"; it is being and must be modified to allow for the growth of "a vaster complex unity . . . founded on universal conditions of human existence."[21]

Now here is the germ of a highly interesting mode of analysis. It would seem—and I think myself this is probably the truth—that variation in ethical standards is not, so to speak, final; that limitations of communication and the absence of common experience provide the source of inability to agree on common justice. Thus, universality is no less a character of the natural law, but it is not within our immediate experience; we cannot tell what ethical goods are universal as between ourselves and some other group of men until we meet that other group as we have met our neighbours. In that case, we cannot hold that universality (or any other character of the Law of Nature) "is not sensible, but rational"; it must be both sensible and rational. Universality is a dynamic force, a power in man's perception of the good that seeks for completion by encountering and assimilating the unknown.

This is what one would like to see developed out of del Vecchio's statement that "the idea of natural law is in fact connected with that of a 'human world-wide law.' "[22] The essential point to concentrate on is that the *idea* or theory of natural law is connected with both the fact and idea of a world society; for if it were merely that natural law in actuality provides standards for all nations, that would be an assertion we know to be incorrect—nor could any such state of affairs come about by an unconscious process. If we were completely to identify natural law with any future set of internationally accepted laws, we should have with us again the confusion between natural law and positive law, only on a larger scale. But one ground of contrast between natural and positive law, and perhaps the most important one, is that the former extends its meaning beyond the area of experience that positive law can in fact or by definition cover, being as it is a temporally and spatially determined record of decisions taken by limited groups. This distinction we should not wish to lose.

No sooner, however, has del Vecchio thrown off these promising hints—and if I am right in reading the direction in which such thoughts could move, there could at the present time be no more exciting or rewarding field of inquiry in the philosophy of law—than he abandons this topic to search for "the logical universal of law, that is ... the form of its idea,"[23] which he says is to be found neither in the natural law's delineation of ideal justice nor in the data of juridical history:

> ... an objective and universal definition of law must have reference only to its form, in other words, to the logical type, which is necessarily inherent in every case of judicial experience, because it is the sign of the possibility of such experience.[24]

Although del Vecchio considers that he has refuted the position of historicists and positivists, he is hardly free from their influence in his insistence that the formal concept of law is not only implied in the knowledge of any juridical fact, but must be "indifferent to and neutral to all juridical principles whatever they are."[25] For a sociologist, this would be an entirely understandable position, perhaps the only position; but for a legal philosopher who holds del Vecchio's views of the ethical standards governing law, it is an anomaly. Del Vecchio is more interested in indicating the possibility of research into the "formal basis of law" than he is in pursuing it very far himself; but the interesting thing is his abandonment of further inquiry into the content of natural law standards, which he first so confidently defends, for the attempt to find a purely formal, ethically neutral definition. In this respect his own thinking shows the continued impact of the historical and positivistic schools.

As one might expect, his search for a purely formal concept leads him into a curious confusion. In the end, he derives the formal definition of law from "the perception of right and wrong, that is the process of reason by which we determine the quality of justice or injustice, right or wrong, conformity or non-conformity to law,"[26] thus equating relationships such as "right-wrong," "conformity or non-conformity to law," which might be thought to be very dissimilar, and assuming as the basis of his inquiry the very notions that it is his task to approach with a purposeful scepticism. It would be futile to point out the inconsistency of this approach with his previous stipulation that the formal definition of law must be ethically neutral, or to show that he has embarked on a line of thought not totally independent of the influence of the Law of Nature, even though merely tangential to it, and lacking all its coherence, as well as its energy and substance.

A more interesting writer than del Vecchio for our purpose is Rudolf Stammler, since his famous formula, "natural law with a variable content," was devised to take into account the omissions and errors in the original, somewhat too optimistic and too simple, versions of the natural law.

Stammler, like del Vecchio, is a neo-Kantian; and the purpose of his *Theory of Justice*[27] is to establish universal formal categories for the determination of just law. Del Vecchio, at least, saw that there is a direct relationship between human experience and the sense of justice; he sought to establish a definition which would be valid for laws of any kind whatsoever, but he did not think this formal definition took the place of an ideal of justice; it was merely intended to be supplementary to it. Stammler conceived that his formal categories would serve not merely to define law but to determine objectively whether or not any given positive law is just. "How can we, in a universally valid manner, determine the justice of a possible content of will which may appear in legal enactments?"[28]

Stammler would like to satisfy the historicists by his admission first of apparently endless variation in the content of specific laws, and second of the way in which changing circumstances may operate so as to nullify the law's intent. At the same time he wishes to retain some general standard of justice having the same function as the Law of Nature but free from its faults. It is Stammler's great merit to see that the Law of Nature is essentially a set of conditions for the making of law or the evaluation of law, and that it should not be thought of as itself a concrete body of laws. "The error of the law of nature," he says,

> lay in the fact that it claimed absolute validity not merely for the method, but also for the material worked up by that method. The fundamental characteristic of concrete legal rules with positive content is that their content is specific material. This peculiarity distinguishes them from principles of method. In a concrete rule of law the specific character of the empirical material is the essential thing; whereas the characteristic of a methodical principle is that it has no such concrete material. Therefore there is in the study of law a universal method, but there are no concrete legal rules whose content is absolutely valid.[29]

Stammler thus seeks to give to a criterion of justice the formal qualities of a logic of law. Here his interest lies close to that of del Vecchio, although, as it has been said, del Vecchio, the less original and substantial thinker of the two, is also the less contradictory.

Stammler's weakness lies in this barren division between form and content—an artificial distinction at best, and particularly bad in this instance, since it leads to a denial that experience enters into the formulation of the abstract standards for justice. His formula, "natural law with a variable content,"[30] was hailed by participants in the revival of natural law as a way out of the awkward dilemma created by the desire to be fully realistic and at the same time to retain the best features of the Law of Nature. But this formula is unsatisfactory precisely because it is a compromise, and suffers from a yawning division between form and content. Stammler's intention is that those laws which have the quality of being objectively just should be considered to be the "content" of natural law. With the passage of time, laws that once were just may come to be unjust, and so the "content" of natural law changes. But the usefulness of the Law of Nature as a set of conditions or standards is destroyed in this analysis. To make positive laws the "content" of the standard obscures the fact that the standard has a content of its own, the substance of the ideal of justice. The ideal of justice can never be made purely formal, like a proposition in logic; but it can be abstracted from specific occasions, and it is none the less lasting or dependable that it has in it the recognizable stuff of experience. In this sense, the content of natural law does not vary.

Perhaps Stammler did not fully see the implications of his suggestion that the Law of Nature is essentially a standard for law. Like the writers of the older treatises, who felt they had to include under the Law of Nature a great many ordinances which they thought belonged to it, Stammler in his turn has to have a content of laws, only they are to remain, as it were, anonymous and unidentified. But if the Law of Nature is understood as a standard, then it has *no* content other than the general criteria of which that standard is composed. One might add that the legal aspect of the Law of Nature is of minor importance compared to its political significance.

Stammler himself apparently sensed some difficulty in his formula; he therefore adopted a slightly different way of working out his essential idea in his *Lehre von dem richtigen Rechte*. Here, in place of the Law of Nature, he gives us his theory of just law, in which the idea of the independence of the standards from all concrete material is preserved.[31] That he is still working out the same problem is demonstrated in the following passage:

> To use our former expression, there is only a law of nature with changing content. There are no specific legal norms whose command is absolutely valid, though it may be objectively just. The conceptual difference between the just and its opposite is absolutely fixed; and the formal method of realizing it in practice is of absolute significance. But the material subject to these conceptions and the specific results determined by them are subject to necessary and inevitable change.[32]

Now there is no difficulty in drawing a distinction between the standards, Law of Nature—or as Stammler would have it, the method—and the material (positive law, statutes, legal enactments) to which the standards are to be applied. But this distinction does not require us to hold that the standards themselves are purely formal. In his striving to outdo Kant, Stammler rejects ethical and political experience as sources of the material for formulating these standards. He says that whereas the seventeenth-century thinkers intended that the Law of Nature should conform to the nature of man, the desirable procedure is to make the Law of Nature express the nature of law. Indeed, he goes so far as to deny that justice has anything to do with experience:

> The concept of justice does not deal with anything that is, or ever will be, experienced in actual life. It deals with a fundamentally formal process by means of which we may be able to apply universal predicates to empirical material.[33]

Further, the act of judging whether a particular legal enactment has the objective quality of just law is not dependent on experience. Stammler himself propounds the question, "For what is it that can tell us that the traditional law is no longer just in its content?"[34] Note, too, that it is the changing of circumstances, of the conditions of life, that acts to render once just law at some later period unjust. One would suppose, then, that it was through a comparison of the standard with one's experience of circumstances that one was able to determine whether the traditional law had become unjust. This, however, is not Stammler's view; he tells us that "the judgment concerning the objective justice of a certain legal content must not be brought in from the outside, but must be derived solely from the imminent [sic] unity of the law itself."[35] Apparently it is only by a pure act of introspection centering on the universal predicates that one can determine where the shoe pinches.

In his criticism of Grotius and the writers following him, Stammler rejects the nature of man as a foundation for law, since, he says, valid deductions cannot be made from a priori notions of the nature of man, in which too much is relative to the philosopher's cast of mind. Likewise, he rejects the *Volksgeist* of the historical school as a cloudy, mystical notion which makes objective criticism of the law impossible. But when we come to discover what he proposes as the all-important universal predicates, we find that he does, in fact, depend on experience. He starts from the idea of "social co-operation as an object of a special kind," and seeks "by critical analysis [to] discover the law imminent in it."[36] He does not see that the notion of social co-operation is open to the same objections that he brings to the idea of man's nature, in that it also has an ethical or empirical foundation and is susceptible of variability in interpretation. His untroubled use of "social co-operation" as a basic notion simply demonstrates that Society rather than Man is now a popular unanalyzable concept.

From the idea that the purpose of law is social regulation Stammler moves on to the formula of "a *community of men willing freely*, as the final expression which comprehends in unitary fashion all possible purposes of persons united under the law. I call this the social ideal."[37] Then he declares that the "definition of the concept, *just legal content*, is the same as that of social unity."[38] The ideal of freedom has already been excluded from the concept of social unity as not being consistent with sovereignty, which is inherent in law. The idea of individual rights is also eliminated, as an offshoot of the cloudy association between the Law of Nature and the nature of man. There is something to be admired, of course, in any attempt to combine in one formula the standpoint of the individual and the aim of the community, whether Kantian in inspiration or not. But it is impossible not to ask where, if not from experience, Stammler has obtained the idea of a community, or of the adjustment of individual purpose in accordance with its needs. When he tells us that "the social ideal demands that the individual should not be forced in his legal relations to renounce his justified interests,"[39] one wonders what the epithet *justified* can mean to him, especially when it is recalled that "the concept of justice does not deal with anything that is, or ever will be, experienced in actual life."[40] Finally, when one arrives after painstaking struggles at Stammler's four universally valid principles for the determination of just law, summed up as the principles of respect and the principles of participation,[41] it is very hard indeed to avoid the feeling that one has met something like these principles before, and that in experience, too. If the principles remind us a little of the Golden Rule as revised by a Prussian Sunday-School teacher, we are still aware of the remote dust of experience nourishing their lean roots; and if every other source fails, it is possible to regard the reading of Kant as also an experience.

In the end, Stammler fails to carry out his own intention (which is really impossible of fulfillment) and his criteria are open to many of the same objections that he has brought against others. His best contribution—beside the vigour with which his argument is conducted—is his clear idea of the Law of Nature as a set of conditions for just law; this we may accept, while rejecting his explanation of the sense and substance of the standards or the way in which they may be derived. We have still with us, then, the question of the content of the Law of Nature and of the place to be made in it for the phenomenon of variability. The use of history as an ethical and political norm has laid a heavy accent on variety and change; but it has given a misleading arrangement to this evidence by restricting its sense either spatially—in the form of nationalism—or temporally, in the substitution of mere logical unity for the substance of justice that lasts through change.

V. THE IDEAL OF JUSTICE IN GOVERNMENT

> ... durable in their main bodies, alterable in their parts.—Sir Thomas Browne, *Urn Burial*.

THE SENSE OF JUSTICE must find its origin in the experience of individuals. The direct knowledge of his own needs which every person acquires is the standard for his admission of the needs of others. The essence of justice consists in the transcendence, through self-knowledge, of our own interests, not in such a manner that they are neglected, but in such a manner that room is created for others as well as ourselves to provide for basic needs. The good of other people must become a value for me, and so enter into the field of my own experience. And hence it must involve a continuous objective reference, so that in the sphere of public affairs "our purposes are directed to ends which in our own consciousness are impartial as to our own interests."[1] This impersonal power of comparison is provided through such an ideal as that of the Law of Nature, with its emphasis on the criteria of consent, of rationality, and of universality.

It will be said that it is impossible to ignore self-interest. But it is neither necessary nor desirable to ignore it. On the contrary, it is only through considering the nature of our own interests that we can imagine what the interests of other people are. By "taking the role of the other," as Meade expresses it, we can advance towards that equilibrium of interests which is the basis for political justice. The difficulty lies, and always will, in generating the initial movement towards transcendence of self-interest. The sense of commonalty in human affairs is partly derived from the experience of mutual interdependence; but it rests also upon an impersonal and objective power of thought. Can we anticipate and to some extent create experience? That is one purpose of a general concept.

It is now time to come back to the central doctrine of the Law of Nature, and to decide whether in its principles we can discern the lineaments of justice today. Coming to it freshly, we can see at once that the labours of the historical school, if they have not built any foundation for the ideal of justice, have left, as a permanent contribution, some important points which we cannot fail to regard. Bearing in mind the four main elements of the Law of Nature theory —the reality, the intelligibility, representativeness, and universality of justice—we might summarize the contribution of the historical school as follows: (1) that the "naturalness" or reality of justice cannot mean that any concrete, prescriptive body of laws can be laid down for all, and that the concept of justice is in part a product of man's development; (2) that justice is not self-evident, and reason does not function automatically, nor, since it is built upon experience, does the use of reason lead everyone to the same conclusions; (3) that consent must operate so as to include widely diverse experience; (4) that the universal is not to be identified with the state of affairs existing at any one time.

Allowing for these corrective readings, to what extent can we depend upon the main elements of the Law of Nature as structural underpinnings of the modern ideal of political justice? We are painfully aware that moral constants which are intrinsically simple in character, are not by that token self-evident. On the contrary, it is often only by hard experience that we can understand the simplest things. We must undertake the not ungrateful task of examining what in some sense we may already be said to know, and it is not an easy kind of inquiry.

The first of the elements which gave to the Law of Nature its force as a political ideal was a belief in the reality of justice. It ought to be clear by now that this belief is a moral perception, independent of scientific or historical knowledge. We do not intend by the term "reality of justice" to imply any exclusive metaphysical or epistemological view, even if, once, in the background of the classic Law of Nature there lurked the shadow of Platonism. Realist or nominalist, monist or pluralist, may join in the recognition of common strains in experience, and that is all that is required. Doubtless no modern writer would assert so confidently as the Stoic a direct connection between the nature of man and an all-embracing moral order to be called "Nature" in the large. Nor would most conscientious modern thinkers ascribe even to their highest intuitions, their strongest feelings of ethical compulsion, the character of Divine Law. Yet if our thoughts of the nature of man are more complicated and our expectations as to his behaviour more modest, can we believe less than that there is a manner of fair dealing and of generosity towards one another which all human beings can understand and value? Believing that, we believe in the reality of justice; and our belief, if different in form, may be linked more closely than we realize to the older Law of Nature school. For to accept so much is to find a large degree of objectivity in what we recognize as good. That manners change is not so fine an observation as the fact that great human virtues can be recognized across the span of time and distance; that there is nothing absolute does not mean that nothing is constant. Although we know that today, as I write and you read, men who deny the meaning of objective justice are at war with half the earth, there can be few who believe that this human failure which we witness and in which we have partaken changes the fact that it is wrong to torture, to starve, and to murder one's fellows, denying their likeness with ourselves.

There can have been, and there will be, no tribe, no kingdom, where all men find it natural to hate and to injure each other. A purpose of co-operation, expressed in institutions no matter how imperfect, is required if men are to live together. The belief that justice belongs to the experience of living, and that it does not perish from the inward eye no matter what outward wrong may be encountered, is built into us as human creatures. That element of the Law of Nature which expresses the reality of justice stands unshaken. It would, doubtless, be possible to cite in favour of it much that psychologists have found. But that is not necessary. Nothing is more dead today than political ideas, like those of James Mill or Bentham, which were hitched too closely to the scientific theories of their time. If ever through any partiality of perspective, schools of science seem to by-pass our deepest moral sense, we had better, like George Eliot, decide "that we must not take every great physicist—or other 'ist—for an apostle, ... if his exposition strands us on results that seem to stultify the most ardent, massive experience of mankind, and hem up the best part of our feelings in stagnation." Indeed, the possibility of scientific knowledge is grounded on intellectual and even ethical constants of the same level as knowledge of the reality of justice.[2]

The second essential element in the doctrine of the Law of Nature was found to be the belief that justice is intelligible, or, as the eighteenth-century writers stated it, the Law of Nature is the Law of Reason. Since then, the champions of irrationalism in various guises have claimed their part as protagonists in the drama of human experience;

but it is still, I think, our resolve and our expectation that affairs shall be governed in a rational manner—difficult as that may prove to be. We no longer think of reason as automatic, it is to us a product of effort; and the "reasonable man" of our jurists (a more comprehensible measure than Reason in the abstract) would not be thought of as too narrowly intellectual. (Let us remember, however, in criticizing the eighteenth-century idea of Reason, that the antithesis then was not between Reason and Emotion or Experience—as it is sometimes stated today—but between Reason and Revelation. It is a distinction that in the realm of politics we shall be wise to hold to.)

An age which lacks spontaneous emotion is ashamed of reason; but there is no antithesis between them. It is impossible to be reasonable without taking account of emotion. Truly thought of, reason is the balanced judgment of a complete person. Man is a being "sensitive, animated, rational"; his self-distrust and his satiric comments upon reason come from reason. When by the operation of intelligence he has detected reason's being partial, when he has seen principle used to express sheer interest, but feignedly (for there is nothing wrong in reason's representing interest when it does so candidly and with clear aim), then he falls into a disillusionment with this, his only instrument of freedom. It is almost impossible to understand how this discrediting of reason can have obtained such hold upon subtle and intelligent men, turning their deepest insights to destructive ends. In many cases this pointing out of the ways in which reason in others has served only as a tool must serve to bolster a sense of superiority in these intellectual arch-detectives. The test is, will they advocate that we should act with deliberate irrationality? If we are not to do so, we must trust reason. Here as in other phases of thought, incomplete self-knowledge has resulted in an inhibition of creative understanding. It is a kind of faith, the faith that life requires, that tells us that what is just must be reasonable even though many actions are justifiably undertaken without rational design. Knowledge has sources in many other aspects of experience. But it is only through reason that we can understand anything for longer than a moment, or can understand the people and the occasions we never directly encounter. Reason, therefore, is an essential bond on any level of social life that seeks to express man's conscious purpose. In politics there can be no justice, no freedom, no democracy without the help of reason.

Still, as before, we are led from the element of rationality to the element of consent. From the fact that justice is intelligible it follows that it *may* be understood by anyone; likewise, that we must welcome every man's contribution to its development. No authority, whether political or ecclesiastical, may claim to be its sole or chief interpreter; no expert, no scientist can be its sole custodian. For by definition it is always ready to be examined, and it cannot be protected from the scrutiny of criticism or the test of conscience. Justice wears its own authority in its character of that which will, because rational, win free assent, and that which, because the best of every one's knowledge and experience can enter into its composition, will be as true as we can make it. The place of consent in the doctrine of the Law of Nature may be expressed as the representativeness of justice.

Now although it is true that decisions arrived at by a majority may in some cases be unjust, and in specific instances the opinions of a minority may be better and wiser, such discrepancies do not show anything wrong with the doctrine of consent. They do, however, disclose something about its relationship with other elements. We know that a majority may, as apparently in Hitler's Germany, prefer tyranny to freedom and may tolerate the worst kinds of cruelty. But if that seems to present a difficulty, the meaning of government by consent is not understood. For government by consent requires the continuous exercise of a method and does not rest on a single act like a plebiscite. Because it is consent and not coercion, it requires not only open and free discussion but respect for the individual person. If the method of consent is accepted, there are at once limitations upon what the majority may do, and the majority agrees to those limitations, which we call "civil liberties." Thus it is not democracy, or government by consent, for a people to vote for tyranny; for the meaning of consent is not fulfilled by voting alone, but only by acceptance of the attitude toward other people and the respect for truth that makes the exercise of consent a continuing possibility.

It remains true, then, that government by the consent of the majority (in the sense explained) is nearer to just government than any alternative that might be proposed. The ideal to aim at in adopting policy, if not in proposing measures for action, may be something close to unanimous consent. But with the interplay of motives, of moods and tempers, the differences in knowledge and experience, the gaps in acquaintance, unanimous consent can rarely be obtained. It is as if unanimous consent were a limiting case, a kind of infinity in politics which the majority's opinion approaches more or less nearly, as the case may be. Majority rule is the calculus of government by consent.

At the same time it is equally true that the opinion of a minority, even of a single individual, may be more in the right, more farseeing, closer to the truth, than the will of the majority. If the minority opinion does come closer to the truth or aim more surely at the good, it represents something not yet understood by many, or a point of change, a growth in knowledge. The justice that lies in minority opinion represents either new knowledge or a more sensitive awareness, greater courage and loyalty. On the other hand, minority opinion may sometimes represent a stubborn loyalty to attitudes or habits or ideas that experience and discovery have made obsolete—this is particularly apt to be true of religious sects or geographically isolated groups. In such cases, it is not the opinion held by the minority that matters but the fact that any number of people sincerely hold it. Thus the state of minority opinion may be the signal, at any given time, either of a group moving forward or of a group that has been left behind or, in times of downfall and destruction, of plain fidelity and courage. As unanimous consent is the limiting case of majority opinion, so the thought of a single individual is the limiting case of minority opinion. In looking forward or in looking backward, minority opinion is the calculus of change upon which all political decisions turn, the margin by which growth in the main direction proceeds, or the discarded experiments which plot the area of accomplishment as surely as iron filings the field of a magnet.

The element of consent then cannot function without the free expression of minority opinion; indeed the very conditions for the forming of majority opinion require the freedom of minorities. For both minorities and majorities are in any given society undetermined; that is, we never know until the time of decision is reached what view the majority will take, what view the minority, or what persons will fall in either category. Where minorities are not free, a true majority cannot be formed. No vote can reflect the choice of a majority if that choice is limited before the vote is taken. The opinions of the minority, or more accurately of minorities, are at any given time the theatre of alternatives from which the majority may later wish to choose. There is, then, no antithesis whatsoever between freedom for the majority and for minorities, although (as with all moving bodies) there is friction. It goes without saying that actual decisions must always, without exception, be taken by the majority. That is the only way in which consent can be obtained. Freedom of opinion for minorities can never mean that they should have the power to rule; that is the point from which we started out. The only way in which consent can be obtained is through agreement to accept the opinion of the majority as decisive of policy; and that is the only protection for minorities as well as for all the rest of the body politic. Were any one minority to govern, no other minority would be safe. The rule of a minority has nothing to do with consent. It is, or it will inevitably become, a rule of force.

Finally, we come to the ideal of the universality of justice. There is no ideal the need of which we know more intimately from our own experience. Like Montaigne, we have seen the justice delivered by the law courts change as men crossed a river or a mountain pass; the possession of a passport mean the way to life, and the lack of it the way to death for the same man, the same moral person.

It was, we found, discovery of the stubborn differences among people and their institutions, and acceptance of these differences as valuable, that led, early in the nineteenth century, to the eclipse of the ideal of universality. That this should have happened shows that critics of the Law of Nature made the same mistake as its eighteenth-century defenders had done: they confused universality with uniformity. What is truly intended by the ideal of universality, of course, is not uniformity but inclusiveness. Were there no differences, there would be no field for universality in which to operate, and were it not possible to look on differences with sympathy, and not to be deterred by them from finding what is common, there would be no good for universality to do.

The ideal of universality is not so much a statement about concrete facts and appearances as it is an indispensable hypothesis for healthy social action and for intelligent use of human energy on any but a localized scale. It lays heavy stress on the qualities that all men share by virtue of being human; it says that the concept of justice is derived from the nature and experience of man and can be no less than universal without being self-contradictory. So conceived, universality will be seen to be a force not denying but demanding change, and continuously transcending the present. At the same time it is a verifiable principle of connection with the past and explains our ability to make any sense out of the art, the religion, the politics, and the philosophy of other generations. If the deeds and the thoughts of men before us have affected the very constitution of our lives and minds, it is so only because general moral, intellectual, and physical capacities cut across all differences of language, geography, and time. Historicism itself, that personification of tradition in its most temporary aspect, that arrested sense of loyalty, that amputated impulse towards union, depends upon the very universality which it distorts and denies. How else but through the sharing of experience and the development of trust within the group can any tribe or nation hang together so as to perpetuate itself? It is the hanging together in experience, the sharing of common good, the acknowledgment of each by the other, that universality asserts without setting any limit to its action.

It might seem that in our own day it is well-nigh impossible to maintain the universality of justice. But are we not the witnesses of the opening scenes of a great drama in which each man, each nation, is being tried by the demand of justice to be universal? And is it not clearer than before that universality means inclusiveness, that men belong to one another? As we read the story of the Poles, the Norwegians, the Yugoslavs—the men in exile and the men in bondage who risk their lives to fan the low spark of liberty, it is not for the loss of their comforts and material possessions that we cry out; it is for the affliction of the human spirit. In them we see ourselves, threatened not with the loss of material goods but of the only good, the right to be fully human, the right to be free. While they have not theirs, we have not our freedom. That is the meaning of universality. Truly, even the persecutors testify to the universal meaning of justice when they use death, torture, confinement, invasion of privacy and suppression of thought as threats and weapons. These are the punishments they bestow, not the rewards they seek. They do not disagree with us about the nature of what, on the simplest level, a man needs and can enjoy. They do disagree about the conditions under which these goods can be obtained without injury to the springs of life within, and they disagree in their sense of who may be included in the group for whom good is designed. In these respects there is none that has not sinned. Our failure has been twofold: we have not, at each stage of advance towards the universality of justice, acted upon what we already know, and we have not yet in our time shaped the image of further advance. In our righteous indignation against all who deny the universality of justice, let us remember the injury—and it is profound—that they do themselves, and have heed to its causes, as well as the will to take away their power.

The universality of justice requires that just law include in its benefits the greatest possible number of people. When for the supposed good of the whole society any are excluded, it must be on the basis of their actual performance as human beings, not on any system of status which shall prejudge them before they have acted. This means that in the light of justice no human beings can be determined to be members of a special class before they are born, and utterly rejects as irrelevant to justice all criteria of race or wealth. Those who may have to be excluded from a free and unlimited participation in social benefits are, like criminals and the insane, wards of society, to be treated with all the sense of responsibility and mercy that that implies. In times of trial the universality of justice has always been denied—as it was, as the whole Law of Nature was attacked, by the defenders of Negro slavery in the Civil War era. This will always be so, for of all the qualities of justice, universality is of the highest level. Acceptance of it requires a generous understanding, and willingness to put it into practice a rare degree of disinterestedness. But without it what humanity have we? No man loves justice who can ignore another's want of it. The universality of justice is the keen edge which it bears against cruelty and oppression; it is the searching light which will test the pride, the selfishness or inertia of any group content with the benefits they have secured. It, and it alone, is the test of whether a man loves anything better than himself.

No final opposition between universality and variability has been disclosed, but the incidence of that factor upon the Law of Nature remains to be considered. This is the peculiarly modern contribution to the ideal of justice, the bearing of diversity upon the essential unity of man. The extent of variation among men has doubtless been exaggerated. But there is still great need to realize that even when people accept the same general aims or standards, their attempts to realize them will be of diverse character, and that this diversity is fruitful and creative, not merely wayward. An intelligent comparison of differences must sharpen our insight into those constants which do not vary. What we may call the ratio of constancy to variability should afford a most interesting area for exploration. We know, for example, that human reactions vary under different conditions. What do we know of the extent to which basic concepts vary under equal conditions? What, to speak more generally, are the constants in respect of which we measure variations? What effect does the untroubled acknowledgment of variation or difference play in bridging apparently diverse customs, thus affording a new sense of common experience?

We need not fear, I think, that the most extensive inquiry into the variety of political ideals will shake the essential elements of justice. The completeness of relativism is an answer to relativism; the possibility that each partial standard (such as nationalism) will itself vary in content with the demands of circumstance, prevents any of the lesser, temporal measures of value from assuming an inherent superiority over the others. (It is for this reason that the ethics of nationalism must inevitably lead to unrestricted competition and to war.) Only the most general elements in such an ideal as justice can be of a higher order; the fact of variability forestalls the claim to grandeur of any variable. Nor, to take another side of the problem, need we see in variation an enemy of rationalism. Reason, indeed, leads towards, not away from, awareness of diversity; for if we acted only upon instinct or emotion, our observation as well as our action would inevitably be more restricted. It is the possibility of transcending immediate experience by generalizing about it which multiplies the possibilities of growth. To generalize is to be susceptible of more incentives, and to perceive more means.

It is my opinion that the principle of variability should be absorbed, with the other elements of the Law of Nature, into our reformulated ideal of justice. The Law of Nature is conceived too narrowly if it does not take account of the relative and the changing as only a general principle can. It has already been indicated that there is no inherent contradiction between universality and variability, if only we have regard to what is universal, and what varies. That certain laws should be universal, and yet changing from place to place, is indeed a contradiction, but there is nothing inconsistent in the view that certain elements of justice are constant, while the attempt to realize these elements in actual life will necessarily take different forms.

Awareness of diversity can operate in either of two contrary ways: it can be interpreted so as to cause defiance and pride, or to suggest humility and moderation. The historicist's conception of the variable, with its linkage to nationalism, has been a narrowing one. Realizing that our own society is not the absolute into which we have erected it should widen the range of our experience; but the method of comparison adopted by the historical school merely substituted a host of parochialisms for the eighteenth century one which, for all its faults, had perhaps been improved by the effort to see it as universal.

A philosophy that sets up variability as a principle superior to, and excluding, the notion of common human values restricts the working of representativeness by cutting off the access of men to each other on a rational level. On the other hand, the broadest possible view of universal humanity allows the character of each individual and each group to contribute its maximum to the composition of the whole society and its ideals. We know a great deal more now than did Herder or Buffon or even Darwin of the variations among physical beings, and we have progressed from a consideration of the variations among groups to the contemplation of individual differences. It is, surely, under a form of government which most nearly assures equal justice to all that the diversity of individuals can be allowed most creative play. Here we find an explanation of the seeming paradox that those political philosophies which deny the common needs of all mankind and deny the reality of justice as a universal ideal in the name of the uniqueness, the separateness of the tribe or national group, force absolute conformity within the group. Thus the working of the principle of variability is nullified if it is not set within the framework of universality. The human attitude that best corresponds with the principle of variability is sympathy, or a willingness to meet and consider the needs of other people; on another level, universality itself leads to the same result.

From the thought that sympathetic understanding of diversity of habit and custom makes an honest acceptance of fundamental equality more possible, two considerations emerge. They are, first, that the use of historical and scientific knowledge lies in making justice concrete; second, that attention to the ratio of constancy and change should lead to a more creative approach to the elements of justice, so that they may be seen as enabling rather than merely enfranchising conditions.

To begin with the first, that the use of scientific and historical knowledge of human variability lies in making justice more concrete. Everyone today must be aware of the disrepute into which great ideals have fallen because, when they were applied without reference to local conditions, their effect was nullified. If, as we go about to establish some state of affairs resting on an ideal of justice, we care nothing for the living tissue of life that we are to encounter, we must be lacking in intelligence or sincerity—and probably both. It is here that the strength of historicism as a tendency embodying the felt need of any national group, or of self-determination on some other scale—for race, class, profession, or individual—enters into the picture. The element of universality in justice demands that we should extend to each group the benefits that are seen as good for man in general. The factor of variability demands that in doing this (since we must always carry out a general aim by a particular action or instrument) we shall take a corrective reading, so that rules which have the appearance of legality but are in a concrete situation unfair to some, shall not be allowed to frustrate our intentions. We must in these cases amend the rule, redesign the instrument, so as to fulfill the general aim more nearly. In this type of problem the factor of variability, far from being antithetical to the element of universality, is really a necessary means towards its fulfillment.

Let us take a simple type of case. "Equality," said Professor Maitland, "has never been so universally accepted an ideal of politics as liberty. Still, it would on all hands be admitted that 'Equality before the law' is good."[3] Well, it is quite true that equality before the law is a widely accepted ideal. It is one that conservatives and liberals can agree on. But a good many conservatives who think they believe in equality before the law are very reluctant to admit that in many cases a workman, an impoverished immigrant, a striker, a Negro, has not had the same protection as the employer, the successful native-born citizen, the white man—either because conditions operated to nullify the intent of the law, or because the specific statutes in question were drawn so as to protect the interests of one group and not of another. Stiff-necked conservatism and refusal to invoke, in such a case, the factor of variability, have operated so as to bring the ideal of justice into disrepute. It is this type of action which gives strength to the communist's relativistic argument that justice (and other social ideals) are merely a projection of the interests of the ruling class. It is this failure of sincerity, this self-righteous lack of interest in the facts on the part of the conservative, that provokes the militant union leader to assert that strikers cannot wait upon the courts for their rights but must win them by their own struggles. It has been, on the international scene, a similar identification of justice with the status quo which has made the exertion of force seem the only way to alter the distribution of power. In each case, the instinct of self-determination has broken through the feeling of loyalty to universal justice. This is likely to happen when "justice" has been used as a cloak for another determining "self" or group.

The most important school of American legal thought today is well aware of the importance of the factor of variability (and that too in conjunction with the other elements of the Law of Nature, whether called that or not). As a consequence we have under way the development of a legal philosophy in which a change in the material conditions of living is recognized as a ground for changes in the interpretation of law, so as to make the law still an instrument of justice. Mr. Justice Cardozo is one who has seen the possibility of retaining the key notions of the Law of Nature and at the same time making place for change. "The outstanding truths of life," he said, "are not to be argued away as myths and vagaries if they do not fit within our little moulds. If necessary, we must re-make the moulds. We must seek a conception of law which realism will accept as true."[4] No eighteenth century writer of the Law of Nature school could have written those sentences. Yet there is an essential continuity of point of view; and the heart of the natural-law theory is not only not lost, it is renewed and given new work to do. Natural law thus becomes the transforming and creative instead of the static and regulative. It is a body of experience absorbed and made articulate by means of general principles; and with a fuller awareness of the "general mixtry of things" it should be far better able to sort them than was the anarchic relativism of the first explorers of the human variable. This happy development of thought, it must be noted, is so far to be seen principally in the realm of jurisprudence. We must hope that once again as in the days of Coke and Blackstone the great lawyers are showing the way for the development of political ideals.

Our second consideration is that the enabling (as distinguished from the enfranchising) conditions of justice are a function of the principle of variability. This relationship rests upon the fact that in studying individual differences we have found so many to arise from insufficiency or deficiency in the essential requirements for human life—food, shelter, the respect of other persons, useful work, leisure. This discloses the typically modern opportunity for the extension of freedom. If we think of the intellectual efforts of the seventeenth- and eighteenth-century thinkers, for example of Milton, Locke, or Jefferson, as devoted to a definition of the enfranchising conditions for justice, to a removal of such barriers to freedom as suppression of thought, political inequality, religious tyranny, irresponsible government, we can think of the modern task as the establishment of the enabling conditions for freedom. "Among these unalienable rights" (or needs for justice) "are life, liberty, and the pursuit of happiness." To that unshaken declaration little need be added; but our knowledge of the enormous variation in the attainment of these ideals even within the folds of democratic society, and our knowledge of the obstacles placed by democratic nations to the attainment of these ideals by other peoples, must increase our resolution to make their meaning for others more concrete than it has ever been. And we can make justice more concrete only by paying honest heed to the diversity of the conditions in which it operates.

Thus the universality of justice requires us to do good to those who are unlike ourselves, and the recognition of their unlikeness as well as the understanding of their needs is an awareness of variability. Awareness of variability is the force that makes universality function in experience. It makes justice more concrete, and joins the enabling to the enfranchising conditions of freedom. The prime political problem of modern times is how to attain the enabling conditions of freedom (or security, as it is popularly called) without sacrificing the enfranchising ones. Freedom to choose, and freedom to do—we need both; the one that our human power may be applied, which is life, the other that our thought and purpose, which is the understanding of life and the quality of it, may direct the application of power.

Seen in this context variability is a factor within all the principles of justice. The belief in universality that leads us to respect the humanity of others, shows us that they will be different from ourselves; belief in the principle of consent requires that a voice must be given to those from whom we differ; the operation of reason is necessary to the belief that they can speak and we can understand. That all the foregoing statements may be read with the same sense if they and we are reversed demonstrates the reality of justice.

The principles of justice are not exercised in a vacuum. They depend upon a rather highly developed community life. They require a state of civilization in which there is respect for the dignity of human beings and regard for truth. The diversity of customs and of institutions is not a barrier to fair dealing. The real barrier that restricts the scope of justice is either ignorance, failure to understand these standards at all, or sheer ill-will and desire for arbitrary power. But because civilization has progressed in uneven stages or because it has tragically relapsed into barbarism is no reason to be apologetic or half-hearted in the support of justice. Its constituent elements, like other valid principles, are adapted to dealing with problems that have *not* been solved. Their function is to create an area of order and fairness within which some attention may safely be paid to more particular and special interests of human beings.

And so the principles of the Law of Nature, or the basic ideals of justice, are both drawn from experience and required for experience. They need no expert to interpret them, and they cannot be resigned to the care of clerk or learned doctor, but must be tested by each individual from the perspective of his share in the common life. Science or history will furnish material again and again for the better understanding of these ideals; at times, in seeming to contradict them, it will furnish the stimulus that makes the ideals grow. For justice, like science, is democratic (although democracy is not scientific and is not always just). As in science the most convincing theory cannot be accepted without test and verification, no matter how great the expert who vouches for it, while, on the other hand, a single man whose opinion is contradicted by the weight of authority may be right, in the same manner the ideals of the Law of Nature are not exhausted by anyone's interpretation of them but are forever demanding from experience a fresh substantiation.

VI. JUSTICE AND POWER

What bearing has discussion of the ideal of universal justice upon our present affairs?

We live at the end of a period of intellectual reaction. For about a hundred years, partly under the influence of German thought, partly under the influence of "social Darwinism," partly under the influence of overspecialization in the world of scholarship and of letters, the ideals of freedom have been eclipsed by the philosophy of might. It is an undeniable historical fact that glorification of force and even of brutality preceded, and did not follow, the onslaught upon civilization attempted in the present century by Germany, Italy, and Japan.

The philosophy of reaction—that is, of denial of value in the brotherhood of man, in reason, and in justice for men of all races and all countries—while at its most dangerous among our enemies, has not been without effect in democratic countries. Before the war broke out, it contributed to the mood of inertia and indifference. It sapped the will to resist. It confused teachers and students, statesmen and citizens. If the ideal of justice was not openly denied, belief in it was weak.

It has been costly indeed to learn that the battles of the past for freedom have not been won. We are fighting not for some as yet unknown benefits for mankind. The plainest, simplest rights are at stake. We see more clearly the importance of economic needs. Yet should we have faltered in the battle, not only would the chance of economic improvement have been lost, but the oldest civil dignities known to man, the tradition of justice and equality that stretches back through Christianity to the Greeks.

In the current debate between "realists" and "idealists" the strength of the intellectual reaction can still be observed. It is perfectly true that some thinkers give insufficient thought to the means by which their ideals may be realized. It is true that sometimes, in their generous wishes for mankind, they stress distant goals and neglect the indispensable first steps without which no progress could be made. Perhaps people of such habits may properly be called, with some sense of their lack of sagacity or of worldly wisdom, "idealists."

But men without ideals are hardly practical or "realistic." For they have no aim, and do not know what they want. In the great debate over the issues of the war and of the post-war period, there is something less than candour in this contrast between "realists" and "idealists". As a rule, the so-called realists are not without ideals. Their ideals—or aims considered worth attaining—are perhaps usually less explicit and are likely to be restricted by a narrowly conceived view of self-interest. They like to say they distrust "abstract" principles. They ridicule an interest in the people of other continents and other races, and the belief that there can be an international association of peoples dedicated to the ideal of justice and prepared to give it power.

A man is truly a realist only if he can take the measure of the world he lives in and find some way to advance towards what he believes to be worth while. It may be money or it may be security for himself and his neighbours; it may be peace for the world or it may be better conditions for labour; it may be success in a profession or it may be leisure;

it may be, and probably is, a combination of several such aims. Being realistic involves something of a gamble. It involves judgment about the state of affairs and understanding of human beings. It is easy for either "realists" or "idealists" to be wrong.

Today it seems the evidence of events, and not any farfetched dream, that the world is slowly becoming one. No nation, with or without "commitments," can live apart from the rest of the world. No nation can hope to avoid war or to succeed in war merely by the possession of military power, without allies. In this situation no man who does not look to the founding of a community of nations governed by law is realistic, unless the goal his policy is adapted to secure be that of nationalism in culture and perpetual war.

Today, as never before, the conditions exist for the concrete testing of the universality of justice. Radio and the airplane have knit the far continents together and have brought all nations into relationship. Whether they will or not, whether or not they have claims over particular bits of territory, nations have been drawn together, and they must learn to live in peace or prepare for anarchy and destruction.

But understanding of the interdependence of nations in the twentieth century will not alone give us the strength and the insight necessary to deal successfully with the situation in which we find ourselves. The crisis of modern times is a moral and intellectual crisis, and recognition of this fact is slowly spreading. In the next few generations, as we strive for the establishment of a world community, our progress will be measured by the degree of our faith in justice for mankind. No machinery, no matter how cleverly devised, will be sufficient to create unity among us. Even peace is not a higher aim than justice, and peace is not worth while at any price. This is not an easy optimism—we know that many individuals and many powerful countries are opposed to the aim of universal justice. We cannot work for this aim without measuring our power with theirs, our willing union with their desperate combination.

We have all become aware of the degree to which international understanding depends upon the solution of major economic problems. But readiness to work for their solution requires a politically informed judgment and is not a problem in economics. The economists have realized this perhaps more clearly than the laymen. "The success of economic measures," says Mr. J. B. Condliffe, "will depend upon the creation of political institutions for the maintenance of peace . . . no discussion of economic problems would be realistic if it omitted such a reminder." And Mr. Eugene Staley, another contemporary economist of distinction, has told us that economic collaboration "must be based on . . . psychological unity." It is in his opinion a great error to underestimate the effect of political factors on economic policy; economic improvement is not to be obtained without the formation of a common will. The mere propinquity of nations and their economic interdependence will not of itself provide people with the motives for coöperation if some deeper sense of unity is lacking.

It is dangerous that some political thinkers should hesitate to identify ideal aims with the structure of world organization. It is true that many so-called "idealists," such as Woodrow Wilson, have not seen clearly the practical measures necessary for the attainment of their aims. They have even confused unsatisfactory practical rules of thumb, such as self-determination, with valid principles such as that of government by consent. But this does not make it the less admirable that they had aims of a universal character. Nor will self-appointed "realists" be successful where men of more willing faith have failed, for the action demanded is of such magnitude that it cannot be carried through without powerful and enduring beliefs.

We sometimes hear that people have become disillusioned with an ideal because some particular action intended to carry it through has failed. This is evidence of a curious immaturity and of failure to understand the function of an ideal or principle. A principle must not be identified with any particular solution of the human problems to which it applies. It directs us what problems to try to solve, and sets standards to which the solution must as nearly as possible conform, but it does not include specific measures—though it may exclude some.

The problems that arise in connection with the exercise of justice are similar to those that arise in giving power to any ideal. They are made inevitable by the task of creating particular conditions to fulfill a general requirement. Since we often do not have control over actual conditions even when we think we know what they should be, the task is very difficult. It goes without saying that the knowledge and skill required to control conditions in the world of human affairs is not given by any ideal alone. It may come from branches of human knowledge such as economics, physics, chemistry, engineering, which are themselves indifferent as to "ends"; or it may come from the practical arts like law or statesmanship, which are necessarily very sensitive to circumstance. But practical knowledge taken by itself, aside from agreement on the aims for which it is to be used, is of very limited benefit to human beings. The techniques of science, of industry, of economics, can be as well used for tyranny as for freedom. The ability of business men, scientists, inventors, generals, may serve a dictatorship as well as a democracy. Taken as engineers or as specialists, there is no difference between the Nazi expert and the American or Englishman. The difference lies in the concept of ends for which a special skill or practical technique is to be used. No amount of practical knowledge will enable man to make the tenor of events reflect his purpose unless he knows what his purpose is, and is ready to make it determine his actions.

The function of such an ideal as that of the Law of Nature was to provide men with an agreed upon statement of purpose in political affairs. By itself, it is neither practical nor impractical, although when once accepted and applied to government, it had a concrete and powerful effect. The eighteenth-century idea of the Law of Nature furnished the layman of that time with a brief description of the conditions of freedom. It endowed his experience and that of every man with validity. It contributed to a unity of thought which is essential to the democratic discipline. It impressed upon every citizen his right to have access to information. It taught men to look beyond the facts of present history to the better world that they might build. Only because its full latitude was not understood did this powerful ideal of a justice common to all men suffer an eclipse. That it should ever have been thought of as supporting prescriptive laws or customs was a contradiction of its essential teaching: that of the freedom of men to govern themselves through the method of consent. In spite of its considerable history this is not an old idea. Attempts to build government upon it are new. The background of our democratic culture, eloquent in the Declaration of Independence or in the strong and modest words of Lincoln, has been permanently enriched by this idea. This is the true moral foundation of a world society. The old terminology of the Law of Nature will not be used again. In its place will stand the more hardly won, the more tempered knowledge of the universal scope of justice.

Belief in the universal scope of justice has very practical consequences. It clarifies our aims in this war. It is founded upon a concept of humanity wide enough to embrace Chinese and Malaysians, Jews and Arabs, Russians and Hindus, as well as Americans and Englishmen. It will not remove the difficulties along the way, difficulties of language, religion, education, customs, and national interests. But it does provide us with a faith by means of which we may hope to reckon honestly with these difficulties and to avoid the morass of despair and cynicism concerning our common future.

When we have an agreed-upon set of aims or values, "a standard," as Washington called it, "to which the wise and honest may repair," we may be as hard-boiled and realistic as we please in trying to build these values into the fabric of common life. We may then well remind ourselves to be modest in our expectations of what can be done in one lifetime. While we study to create the absolute essentials of cooperation among men and nations willing to accept the ideal of justice and of law—and these will be in the near future only some nations—we may be wise to refuse a "dissipated philanthropy."[1] We must learn not to cast away the gains we are able to make because there are others towards which the way is not clear. Once we have chosen our targets and set the sights, we had better be ready for many difficulties and some failures. But that is no reason to abandon the objective.

We may conclude, then, that there is nothing impractical in an attempt to reach an agreement on general principles, but that on the contrary, without such agreement, without unity of thought on basic aims, concrete specific measures or mere tactics will produce nothing but uncertainty and friction. The popular battle between "idealists" and "realists" is partly only an epidemic of slogans and name-calling, partly an unconscious demonstration of the effect of the intellectual reaction whose initial stages have been described in this book.

Once agreement exists on fundamental objectives (whether in the ancient form of natural law or the modern shorthand of the Four Freedoms) it is a moral obligation as well as a practical necessity to be as concrete as possible about how they may be implemented. And here it is well to remember that different alternative means are possible, that circumstances have always to be considered, but that the nature of the goal will help by clearly ruling out some proposals for action and indicating others as the *sine qua non* of further progress. To give an example: it is perfectly clear to a believer in these ideals today that the absolute prerequisite of further advance towards the establishment of justice is the founding of an organization of nations which transcends national, regional, and racial barriers. Although it will probably not be possible to include all nations within it at first, that should be the eventual goal. To do any good, such an organization must endure, and we are therefore led to look for a type of association which will be consistent with government by consent and yet coherent enough to take real decisions. It does not take much imagination to see that if the degree of union we already have, in the United Nations, is allowed to fall apart in the period after the war, it will be perhaps impossible, in the chaos that might follow, to recover even the inadequate degree of co-operation that we now have. Therefore, the practical conclusion indicated is to start on the foundation of the United Nations.

The mere declaration of principles without intention to act upon them brings political ideals into disrepute. "Not to act on our beliefs, is often equivalent to acting as if the opposite beliefs were true."[2] Could there be any more vivid illustration of this than American foreign policy between the two wars? The recent White Paper of the U.S. State Department[3] is the most clinching demonstration of the unreadiness of the American people to give any practical support to their announced ideals. Nothing could be more disheartening than this honest record of a decade during which the declaration of principles was futile, not because the principles were bad, but because the offenders knew there was no intention to take action. The fault was not primarily in the State Department but in the thinking and behaviour of the people. A situation of this kind makes the enunciation of principles seem a pious sham. The same reason accounts for the utter unreality to the average citizen of international law. The widespread demand for an international organization to be backed up by force is an admission that principles require action. In the absence of a willingness to provide measures of enforcement, an instrument like the Kellogg pact serves only to bring discredit upon the principles it declares. It opens the door to insincerity on the part of its opponents and to disillusionment on the part of its well-meaning sponsors. Provisions for the enforcement of law show an unmistakable intention that the principles regarded as fundamental to the common good shall be translated into reality. The attainment of a real United Nations organization, however limited, would do more to awaken in the hearts of all men a belief in world justice than any number of official speeches or diplomatic negotiations.

For justice is a practical virtue, it represents the desire to express in living the virtues that we contemplate in the mind. It is a continuing direction, not a remote end. The practice of it is the only way of knowing it. Known and acted upon, it is the invigorating tonic of actual life, no Utopia to be sought in dreams and disowned in disillusion. The mistaken idea that an ideal state of things can be discovered and maintained saps the intelligence. It confuses the conditions for just action, which we can know, with some final solution of human problems, which is beyond our power.

There are certain concepts the meaning of which can not be expressed by seeking and obtaining another set. Truth is one of them, goodness another. Justice, however, is probably of a level of abstraction inferior to these. It has a relation to truth and a relation to goodness. In practice, it is the result obtained by acting in accordance with the principles which most nearly combine sympathy for human nature, objectivity of reference, and relevance to social need. As such it is only a rough product. For these principles do not always work in the same direction or indicate the same decision.

Justice, then, is not identical with the good, but the most just action is an action undertaken with nothing but the good in mind. It falls short of the good by the limits imposed by lack of knowledge and lack of power. Justice is the learned, as opposed to the given, aspect of goodness. It is the method that puts into practice what we can understand, what, if you will, we can manage, of love, of goodness, among men. But what we can understand and what we can manage without too great loss may not be adequate. These practical methods are like the surgeon's splints, not the healing itself, not the new life.

Justice is never wholly equal to goodness. But goodness is not wholly appropriate for social direction. It is too diffuse, too extensive, its implication for the whole of life is greater than our perception of it. Justice marks the way we learn to know, the dikes, the Roman road; love or goodness is broader, goes farther, but except as it may purely and uniquely enter individual perception, it is not definitely directive of the concrete. We may see it and hold it higher than all else. But meanwhile there is the jungle, there are irresistible facts, and the social complex is not to be charmed or converted. It is to be dealt with by action, not by contemplation.

Say that justice lies in the realm of knowledge, not being. It is therefore imperfect. But it is amenable to control, to testing, and it can be made clear to other minds. By nature it is in need of improvement and therefore it has constant interest as well as merit.

NOTES

NOTES TO CHAPTER II

1 The principle of the natural equality of all men, "that all men are born free and equal," affirms that status is not a part of the human constitution. It does not mean, as some of its critics have assumed, that all are equal in ability, strength, or energy. Criticism directed at this mistaken view is beside the point and fails to impair the essential truth that there is no distinguishing edict of nature by which one man is born a noble and another a serf, one a captain of industry and another a sharecropper. For Locke's description of equality, see *Two Treatises of Government* (Everyman ed.), pp. 118, 142. Jefferson's expression is clear enough: "The mass of mankind has not been born with saddles on their backs, nor a favored few booted and spurred, ready to ride them legitimately, by the grace of God."

2 Sir Frederick Pollock, "The History of the Law of Nature," in *Essays in the Law* (London, 1922), p. 20.

3 Charles G. Haines, *The Revival of Natural Law Concepts* (Cambridge, Mass., 1930), p. 20.

4 Cicero, *On the Commonwealth* (trans. with Notes and Introduction by George Holland Sabine and Stanley Barney Smith, Columbus, Ohio, 1929), Introduction, p. 22.

5 *Ibid.*, p. 31.

6 It is most difficult to distinguish sharply between the Law of Nature as a political and as a legal concept, especially when one thinks of the political endeavours of seventeenth-century lawyers or of the legal training of political philosophers. There is an inevitable overlapping of political and legal theory as soon as problems concerning the derivation of authority are considered. But if it is clear that the Law of Nature had a legal history before it became of political importance, it must be equally plain that when legal notions begin to have a political effect they may be legitimately considered from the political point of view, without ref-

erence to the subtleties that determine what the courts will enforce. Such problems as the relation of a "higher law" to the declared will of a supposed sovereign have received attention from a long list of writers to whom Coke and Blackstone, among others, gave abundant opportunity.

7 No single authoritative history of the Law of Nature can be cited. The following books and articles are useful as furnishing an introduction to the historical study of this concept: E. Burle, *Essai historique sur le développement de la notion de droit naturel dans l'antiquité grecque* (Trévoux, 1908); George Holland Sabine and Stanley Barney Smith, Introduction to *On the Commonwealth;* H. F. Jolowizc, *Historical Introduction to the Study of Roman Law* (Cambridge, 1932), Ch. VI: "Law for Foreigners, *ius gentium* and *ius naturale*"; R. W. and A. J. Carlyle, *A History of Mediaeval Political Theory in the West* (6 vols., Edinburgh and London, 1903-1936); Otto von Gierke, *Political Theories of the Middle Ages* (trans. by F. W. Maitland, Cambridge, 1922), *The Development of Political Theory* (trans. by Bernard Freyd, New York, 1939), and *Natural Law and the Theory of Society* (trans. by Ernest Barker, 2 vols., Cambridge, 1934); James Bryce, "The Law of Nature," in *Studies in Jurisprudence* (2 vols., New York, 1901), Vol. II; Sir Frederick Pollock, *op. cit.;* Charles G. Haines, *op. cit.;* Benjamin F. Wright, *American Interpretations of Natural Law* (Cambridge, Mass., 1931); Morris Cohen, "Ius Naturale Redivivum," *Philosophical Review,* XXV (1916), 761ff.; Roscoe Pound, *The Spirit of the Common Law* (Boston, 1921), *An Introduction to the Philosophy of Law* (New Haven, 1922), and *Interpretations of Legal History* (New York, 1923); Edward S. Corwin, "The 'Higher Law' Background of American Constitutional Law," *Harvard Law Review,* XLII (1928-1929), 149ff., 365ff.; J. Charmont, *La Renaissance du droit naturel* (Montpelier, 1910). Consult also C. H. McIlwain, *The High Court of Parliament and its Supremacy* (New Haven, 1910). Many of the works of Continental writers participating in the "revival" of natural-law theory are reprinted in the Modern Legal Philosophy Series.

8 Locke, *op. cit.,* pp. 119, 143.

9 *Ibid.,* p. 127.

10 For the ideas of the Levellers see the Putney Debates in A. S. P. Woodhouse, *Puritanism and Liberty* (London, 1938); cf. also T. C. Pease, *The Leveller Movement* (Washington, D. C., 1916).

11 Locke, *op. cit.,* pp. 184-85.

12 John Adams, *Works* (Boston, 1856), X, 282.

13 J. C. Miller, *Sam Adams* (Boston, 1936), p. 90.

14 Adams, *op. cit.,* X, 275. Otis, John Adams says in this letter, was "a great master of the laws of nature and nations. He had read Pufendorf, Grotius, Barbeyrac, Burlamaqui, Vattel, Heineccius."

15 Thomas Paine, *The Rights of Man,* Bk. II.

16 Justice can be thought of as a requirement of human nature, so that the Law of Nature is derived from the nature of man, or as given by the laws that govern all created nature, and hence either a command of God or a law so perfectly expressive of divine goodness and wisdom that God

could not contradict it without contradicting himself. In either case we are dealing with an article of faith, the faith that Justice is.

17 Christian Wolff, for example, claimed for his work on natural law the certitude of mathematics. "Tout cela ne pouvait donc être mis en plein jour qu'en suivant les traces d'Euclide, rigide observateur des loix d'une saine logique, c'est à dire en expliquant chaque terme par un définition exact, . . . et en rangeant soit les définitions, de façon que les précédentes fissent pleinement entendre les suivantes, soit les propositions, de façon que la verité de chacune parut par celles qui les précédent."
—*Institutions du Droit de la Nature* (traduites du Latin . . . par Mr. M., 2 vols. in 1, Leyde, 1772), p. v.

18 "The general and perpetual voice of men is as the sentence of God himself."—Hooker, *Laws of Ecclesiastical Polity*, Bk. I, ch. viii, sec. 3.

19 Cicero, *De Republica*, III, xxi, 33.

20 Montaigne, *Essais* II, xii. Pascal, who also despaired of universal justice (but more bitterly), has turned this passage to his own use: "On what shall man found the order of the world which he would govern? . . . Shall it be on justice? Man is ignorant of it. Certainly, had he known it, he would not have established this maxim, the most general of all that obtain among men, that each should follow the customs of his own country. The glory of true equity would have brought all nations under its sway, and legislators would not have taken the fancies of the Persians and Germans as their model, instead of this unchanging justice. We should have seen justice established in all the states of the world and in all periods, whereas we see neither justice nor injustice which does not change in quality with change in climate. Three degrees of latitude reverse the whole of jurisprudence; a meridian decides what truth is; . . . right has its epochs, the entry of Saturn into the Lion marks out for us the origin of such and such a crime. A curious justice that is bounded by a river! Truth on this side of the Pyrenees, error on the other side."
—Blaise Pascal, *Oeuvres Complètes* (ed. by Fortunat Strowski, Paris, 1926-1931), III, 142.

21 The view of the Law of Nature put forth by such writers as Hobbes and Spinoza, in spite of its great intrinsic interest, most certainly does not belong to the main tradition of the concept and is therefore excluded from this discussion. In any full historical study it would have to be considered—as, perhaps, a "naturalistic" law of nature! Cf. Heineccius' remark that Hobbes's purpose is to subvert the Law of Nature and that his use of the term can only be intended to confuse (Heineccius, *A Methodical System of the Universal Law*, trans. by George Turnbull, 2 vols., London, 1763, I, 49). Though this remark shows a clear misunderstanding of Hobbes, it is nevertheless evidence that writers in the main tradition recognized that Hobbes rejected the premises which were commonly recognized as fundamental. It may be argued, from the point of view of the semanticist, that "Law of Nature" is a term to which many different meanings have been attached; this is true, but it does not alter the fact that the main lines of development of the doctrine stressed the elements here enumerated and that it was this version which had political influence.

22 The lack of clarity in some writers on this point doubtless goes back to the vagueness of the Romans on the distinction between *ius gentium* and *ius naturale*. In the process of building the *ius gentium*, recourse was had, among other sources, to those simple rules of equity recognized by the people of many different nations, and thus consent or agreement of a kind that could be empirically determined was taken to be an aspect of the *ius gentium*. The notion of consent that is implicit in the Stoic doctrine of the natural law is of a somewhat different character; it arises from the conception of the nature of man and is not to be thought of as depending primarily upon empirical verification. The blending of the notions of *ius gentium* and *ius naturale* tended to blur the distinction at the same time that it enriched the meaning of the element of consent. (Cf. Bryce, *op. cit.*, II, 570ff., for a good summary of the texts and practices that illuminate the relationship between these terms.) Grotius, in taking up the importance to be attached to general agreement or consent, tries to make a distinction between the Law of Nature as based upon a priori, analytical reasoning, and the Law of Nations as based upon empirical evidence: ". . . when many at different times, and in different places, affirm the same thing as certain, that ought to be referred to a universal cause; and this cause, in the lines of inquiry we are following, must be either a correct conclusion drawn from the principles of nature, or common consent. The former points to the law of nature, the latter, to the law of nations." Proof a posteriori, he continues, is of limited use in bringing us to the knowledge of what is in accord with the law of nature, although it may justify us in concluding "if not with absolute assurance, at least with every probability, that that is according to the law of nature which is believed to be such among all nations, or among all those which are more advanced in civilization." After citing Hesiod, Aristotle, Cicero and others to the effect that common agreement is a criterion of the Law of Nature, he adds: "Not without reason did I speak of the nations 'more advanced in civilization'; for as Porphyry rightly observes, 'Some nations have become savage and inhuman, and from them it is by no means necessary that fair judges draw a conclusion unfavourable to human nature.'"—*De Iure Belli ac Pacis* (trans. by F. W. Kelsey, Carnegie Endowment for International Peace, 1925), II, 23-24, 42-43.

Heineccius, writing later than Grotius, and perhaps more aware of the increased interest in social facts, refuses the loophole offered by the criterion of advanced civilization and sets aside altogether the appeal to consent. He argues that consent, where it exists, is not at first evident to all men as the Law of Nature must be, secondly that what all nations agree on is not necessarily conformable to the divine will, finally that there is not in fact sufficient agreement among nations on such important matters as religion and marriage laws. He concludes that it is not "the consent of all nations or of all civilized nations" that gives us the principle of natural law. But most writers on this subject do give a considerable place to the element of consent, and in the popular mind it was of great importance.

23 The meaning of the element of variability and its place among the elements of the Law of Nature concept will be discussed in Chapter III; and the difference between this method of analysis and Stammler's "natural law with a variable content" will, I hope, become clear.

24 Cf. A. O. Lovejoy, "Pride in Eighteenth Century Thought," *Mod. Lang. Notes*, XXXVI (1921), 31ff.; "The Discrimination of Romanticisms," *P.M.L.A.*, XXXIV (1924), 299ff.; "Optimism and Romanticism," *P.M.L.A.*, XLII (1927), 921ff.; "The Meaning of Romanticism for the Historian of Ideas," *Jour. Hist. Ideas*, II (June, 1941), 257ff. Cf. also *The Great Chain of Being* (Cambridge, Mass., 1936).

25 See, however, Geoffroy Atkinson, *Les Nouveaux Horizons de la Renaissance Française* (Paris, 1935), and *Les Relations des Voyages du XVII Siècle et l'Évolution des Idées* (Paris, n.d.) for an excellent summary and analysis of material bearing on this problem.

26 A few words from the letter of a Brazilian Jesuit, Père Nobrega, will illustrate the confusion of the two ideas: "En plusieurs choses ils gardent la loi de la nature: ils n'ont rien de propres, tout leur est commun," etc. (quoted in Atkinson, *Les Nouveaux Horizons de la Renaissance Française*, p. 143).

27 *Ibid.*, p. 392.

28 Montaigne, *Essais*, III, vi, 882.

29 The voyages of Dampier, Bougainville and others of course contributed to knowledge of these parts of the world. Cook's explorations were, however, the climax of this era of discovery; the concreteness of detail and the dramatic effect of the narrative put the relations of his voyages beyond comparison.

30 Darwin, *The Descent of Man*, in *The Origin of Species* and *The Descent of Man* (Mod. Library ed.), p. 919.

NOTES TO CHAPTER III

1 Edmund Wilson, *To the Finland Station* (New York, 1940), p. 3.

2 Cf. Lovejoy, *The Great Chain of Being*.

3 Carl Becker's *The Heavenly City of the Eighteenth Century Philosophers* (New Haven, 1932) is a most interesting study of the worship of history as embedded in the future.

4 Benedetto Croce, *The Philosophy of Giambattista Vico* (trans. by R. G. Collingwood, London and New York, 1913), pp. 107-8.

5 *Ibid.*, p. 104.

6 *La Scienza Nuova, giusta l'edizione del 1744, a cura di Fausto Nicolini* (Bari, 1928), II, 162. The *Scienza Nuova* exists in two French translations: one, an abridged version, by J. B. Michelet (*Principes de la Philosophie de l'Histoire, traduits de la Scienza Nuova de J. B. Vico*, Paris 1827); the other by the Countess Belgiojoso (*La Science Nouvelle, par Vico, traduit par l'auteur de l'essai sur la Formation du Dogme Catholique*, Paris, 1844). It has never been translated into English.

7 *Scienza Nuova*, II, 72.
8 *Ibid.*, II, 67.
9 At times Vico uses the expression "natural law" as equivalent with sociability. Writers of the natural-law school have been criticized for a view of human society that is too "atomistic," but many of them, for example Grotius and Pufendorf, gave prominence to "sociability," and Vico is probably echoing Grotius. Cf. *Scienza Nuova*, I, 76.
10 Michelet, *op cit.*, Introduction, p. 31.
11 *Scienza Nuova*, II, 57.
12 Croce, *op. cit.*, p. 60.
13 *Scienza Nuova*, I, 81.
14 *Discourse on Method* in *Philosophical Works* (trans. by Elizabeth S. Haldane and G. R. T. Ross, 2 vols., Cambridge, 1911-1912), I, 82-83.
15 *Scienza Nuova*, I, 77. The phrase *senso commune* as used by Vico is nearer to "collective consciousness" or "communal sense" than to "common sense."
16 *Ibid.*, I, 118.
17 *Ibid.*, I, 121.
18 *Ibid.*, II, 158.
19 Croce, *op. cit.*, p. 5.
20 *Scienza Nuova*, I, 117: "Ma, in tal densa notta di tenebre ond' è coverta la prima da noi lontanissima antichitá, apparisce questo lume eterno, che non tramonta, di questa veritá, la quale non si può a patto alcuno chiamar in dubbio: che *questo mondo civile egli certamente è stato fatto degli uomini.*"
21 *Ibid.*
22 *Ibid.*, I, 86.
23 Croce, *op. cit.*, p. 65.
24 *Ibid.*, p. 19.
25 Sorel was, as a matter of fact, acquainted with the *Scienza Nuova*. See Croce, *op. cit.*, p. 277 (App. II).
26 Cf. O. von Gemmingen, *Vico, Hamann und Herder* (Dissertation, Leipzig, 1918).
27 These details are taken from Croce, *op. cit.*, App. II, in which a much fuller account is given of Vico's possible influence on later writers.
28 P. Flourens, *Buffon, Histoire de ses Travaux et de ses Idées* (Paris, 1844), p. 165.
29 From *Le Verger des Charmettes*. For an account of popular interest in natural history in eighteenth-century France, cf. Daniel Mornet, *Les Sciences de la Nature en France au XVIII Siècle* (Paris, 1911).
30 *Oeuvres Complètes de Buffon* (mise en ordre ... par M. le Comte de Lacepède, Paris, 1817), I, 30. For the sake of convenience all citations in this chapter have been made from the Lacepède edition; the best edition is the original one, *Histoire Naturelle générale et particulière* ... (Paris, Imprimerie Royale, 1749-1788).
31 Buffon, *Oeuvres Complètes*, I, 31.
32 *Ibid.*, VI, 219.
33 *Ibid.*, IV, 417.

34 That is, from the work of Adam Smith and Malthus. That Darwin found in Malthus the initial suggestion for his idea of the struggle for existence is well known. Malthus himself draws support from natural history in his assumption that overcrowding is inevitable: "Through the animal and vegetable kingdoms, nature has scattered the seeds of life abroad with the most profuse and liberal hand. She has been comparatively sparing in the room, and the nourishment necessary to rear them. The germs of existence contained in this spot of earth, with ample food, and ample room to expand in, would fill millions of worlds in the course of a few thousand years. Necessity, that imperious all-pervading law of nature, restrains them within the prescribed bounds. The race of plants, and the race of animals shrink under this great restrictive law. And the race of man cannot, by any efforts of reason, escape from it."—*First Essay on Population, 1798* (Facsimile Reprint for the Royal Economic Society), p. 15. Malthus continues, "Among plants and animals the view of the subject is simple. They are all impelled by a powerful instinct to the increase of their species; and this instinct is interrupted by no reasoning, or doubts about providing for their offspring. Wherever therefore there is liberty, the power of increase is exerted, and the superabundant effects are repressed afterwards by want of room and nourishment, which is common to animals and plants, and among animals, by becoming the prey of others."—*Ibid.*, p. 27. Among humans the effect of this check on population is more complicated; but one method by which the struggle for existence operates is through war: "An Alaric, an Attila or a Zingis Khan, and the chiefs around them, might fight for glory, for the fame of extensive conquests; but the true cause that set in motion the great tide of modern migration, and that continued to propel it till it rolled at different periods, against China, Persia, Italy, and even Egypt, was a scarcity of food, and a population extended beyond the means of supporting it."—*Ibid.*, pp. 49-50. Thus *Lebensraum* in 1798! But to Malthus "the commission of war is vice" and "the struggle for existence" does not make it good (p. 52). Note the form of the reasoning: (1) overcrowding or abundance leads to (2) insufficiency of room or food and (3) reason is apparently unable to cope with necessity so that (4) a struggle for existence taking the most destructive forms is the "natural" result.

35 Buffon, *op. cit.*, VI, 276-77. Add to this "qu'il devrait être indifférent à la nature que telle espèce détruisit plus ou moins" and one of the chief tenets of the Nazi ideology is already fashioned, if not yet available for use. See Vol. I, "Théorie de la Terre," and compare also his "Essai d'un Arithmétique Morale."

36 *Ibid.*, I, 32.

37 Blumenbach, *De Generis Humani Varietate Nativa Liber* (1st ed. Goettingen, 1775, reprinted in *The Anthropological Treatises of Blumenbach*, trans. by Thomas Bendyshe, London, 1865).

Linnaeus really belongs among the monogenists although his views were modified in later editions of his work. In the first edition of the *Systema Naturae* (1735) he classed man among the animals, order Anthropomorpha, and found but one species of man to which the various races belonged. But in the tenth edition (1758) he lists *homo nocturnus*, the orang-outang, as forming a second species. *Homo ferus*, the wild man, appears as a variety of *homo sapiens*. Patagonians and Hottentots are included among the examples of wild men.

38 Buffon, *op. cit.*, VII, 1.

39 *Ibid.*, II, 527. Cf. V, 344ff. (Addition à l'article des variétés de l'espèce humaine: "Insulaires de la mer du Sud," and "Habitans des Terres Australes"). This whole article, one of the supplements to the original edition of the *Histoire Naturelle*, is interesting particularly for Buffon's comment on the importance of Cook's voyages for the study of man. In the original section to which this is a supplement he had drawn his information from the material published by Dutch travellers to the East Indies and from Dampier. The revision was considered necessary in order to take account of the discoveries of Bougainville and Cook: "M. Cook, qui, lui seul, a plus fait de découvertes que tous les Navigateurs qui l'ont precédé" (V, 349).

40 *Ibid.*, VII, 97 ("De la Nature, Seconde Vue"). Cf. "The nation in an organism embracing an indefinite series of generations in which the individual is but a transient element" (Programme of the National Fascist Party, December 1921). "The Italian nation is an organism endowed with purposes, a life and means of action transcending in power and duration, those of the separate individuals or groups of individuals which compose it." (Article I of the Italian Charter of Labor, 1927, reprinted in Welk, *Fascist Economic Policy*, Cambridge, Mass., 1938, App. I.) ". . . Nature concentrates, not on safeguarding that which exists, but on breeding the coming generation as the representative of the species." (Adolf Hitler, *Mein Kampf*, Reynal and Hitchcock, New York, 1939, p. 39.)

41 Buffon, *op. cit.*, I, 47.

42 *Ibid.*, V, 5.

43 *Ibid.*, I, 42.

44 *Ibid.*, IV, 414-15. It is quite possible that Buffon's views on this subject did change in the course of the many years during which the volumes of the *Histoire Naturelle* were being written and published. In the earlier portion he is anxious to dispose of the Linnaean classification, which he thought too artificial. There, it is the notion of the *fixity* of species he would like to get rid of; species melt into varieties; there are so many shades and nuances of difference that hard and fast distinctions cannot be drawn. In the later passage it is the persistence in time of a collective entity, an idea in the Workmaster's mind, that he is trying to describe. There is obviously the influence of Platonism to reckon with. Yet I think it possible, also, that Buffon had come to modify his earlier attitude toward this subject. "De la manière d'étudier . . . l'histoire naturelle" appeared in the first volume of his work in 1749; "De la Nature Seconde Vue" appeared in the seventh volume in 1765. Buffon's account of changes in the earth underwent a change between the publication of "Théorie de la Terre" in 1749 and of "Époques de la Nature" in 1778. Cf. Flourens, *op. cit.*, for a compact summary of the differences between these two **treatises.**

NOTES TO PAGES 54-64

45 Buffon, *op. cit.*, VII, 98.
46 And these pale panting multitudes
   Seen surging here, their moils, their moods,
   All shall "fulfil their joy" in Thee
   In Thee abide eternally!
   (*The Dynasts*, Part III, After Scene)
47 Buffon, *op. cit.*, VII, 101-2.
48 Herder, *Sämmtliche Werke* (herausgegeben von Bernhard Suphan, Berlin, 1887-1917), Vols. XIII and XIV. All citations are from the Suphan edition. The translations are in the main taken from Churchill (*Outlines of a Philosophy of the History of Man*, trans. from the German of John Godfrey Herder . . . by T. Churchill, 2nd ed. in 2 vols., London, 1803), which, since it is an almost contemporary translation, preserves something of the spirit of the original. Where Churchill fails to bring out something important in the sense of a passage, I have made my own translation. References are given for all the passages taken from Churchill; the others may be assumed to be mine. The *Ideen* was also translated into French by Edgar Quinet (*Idées sur la Philosophie de l'Histoire de l'Humanité*, 3 vols., Paris, 1827).
49 Herder, *op. cit.*, XIII, 60.
50 *Ibid.*, XIII, 55-56.
51 *Ibid.*, XIII, 255.
52 *Ibid*, XIII, 257 (Churchill, I, 298).
53 *Ibid.*, XIII, 258 (Churchill, I, 298).
54 *Ibid.*, XIII, 345.
55 *Ibid.*, XIII, 56-57.
56 *Ibid.*, XIII, 259.
57 *Ibid.*, XIII, 63 (Churchill, I, 64).
58 *Ibid.*, XIII, 218 (Churchill, I, 248).
59 *Ibid.*, XIII, 235: "Mit dieser Oelreichen Organisation zur sinnlichen Wohllust." The happily literal translation is from Churchill (I, 270).
60 *Ibid.*, XIII, 236 (Churchill, I, 271). It should be noted in connection with the question raised here that Herder does not question Camper's use of "facial angles" as an index of the superiority or inferiority of types of men (Bk. IV, Ch. II).
61 *Ibid.*, XIII, 196.
62 Cf. Bk. IV, Ch. IV.
63 Herder, *op. cit.*, XIII, 148.
64 *Ibid.*, XIII, 351.
65 *Ibid.*, XIII, 147-48 (Churchill, I, 164-65).
66 *Ibid.*, p. 147 (Churchill, I, 164).
67 *Ibid.*, pp. 257-58 (Churchill, I, 298).
68 Robert R. Ergang, *Herder and the Foundations of German Nationalism* (Columbia Univ. Studies in History, Economics and Public Law, no. 341, 1931), p. 84.
69 *Ibid.*, pp. 248-49.
70 Herder, *op. cit.*, XIV, 31.
71 Cf. Adam Ferguson: ". . . both the earliest and latest accounts col-

lected from every quarter of the earth represent mankind as assembled in troops and companies." Accordingly, "Mankind are to be taken in groups, as they have always subsisted. The history of the individual is but a detail of the sentiments and the thoughts he has entertained in the view of his species: and every experiment relative to this subject should be made with entire societies and not single men."—*Essay on the History of Civil Society*. I am indebted for these passages to Professor Gladys Bryson of Smith College. They are quoted in Chapter II of her unpublished study, The Philosophical Background of the Social Sciences.

72 Herder, *op. cit.*, XIII, 339, quoted in Ergang, *op. cit.*, Dr. Ergang points out Stein's use of this passage.

73 See *Ideen*, Bk. XVI, Chs. III and VI (*op. cit.*, XIV).

74 Herder, *op. cit.*, XIII, 18 (Churchill, I, 8).

75 *Ibid.*, XIII, 299.

76 *Ibid.*, XIII, 303.

77 *Ibid.*, XIII, 309 (Churchill, I, 362).

78 *Ibid.*, XIII, 339.

79 *Ibid.*, XIII, 393 (Churchill, I, 459).

80 *Ibid.*, XIII, 348 (Churchill, I, 410).

81 *Ibid.*

82 Hans Kohn, *Force or Reason* (Cambridge, Mass., 1937), p. 60.

83 Herder, *op. cit.*, XIII, 345.

84 *Ibid.*, XIII, 392 (Churchill, I, 457). An incident related in Cook is an amusing illustration of how the importance of burial customs was in one instance impressed upon the explorers. As Cook was about to take leave of the people of the Society Islands on his second voyage, "Oreo pressed him to return; when the captain declined making any promises on that head, he asked the name of his morai (burying-place). As strange a question as this was, he hesitated not a moment to tell him Stepney, the parish in which he lived when in London. He was requested to repeat it several times over till they could pronounce it; then 'Stepney morai no Toote' was echoed through a hundred mouths at once. What greater proof could they have of these people esteeming them as friends, than their wishing to remember them even beyond the grave?"—*Captain Cook's Voyages of Discovery* (Everyman ed., pp. 176-77).

85 *The Will to Power*, aphorisms 1,005 and 462.

86 Herder, *op. cit.*, XIII, 24 (Churchill, I, 16).

87 *Ibid.*, XIII, 353 (Churchill, I, 416). Cf. also *Ideen*, Bk. XV, Ch. II (*op. cit.*, XIV).

88 *Ibid.*, XIII, 54.

89 *Ibid.*, XIV, 85-86.

90 *Ibid.*, XIII, 350 (Churchill, I, 415).

91 *Ibid.*, XIII, 381.

NOTES TO CHAPTER IV

1 Hume, *An Inquiry Concerning the Principles of Morals*, App. III.
2 Cohen, "Ius Naturale Redivivum," *The Philosophical Review*, XXV, 765.
3 Cf. Pound, *The Spirit of the Common Law*. The same point of view is maintained in Professor Pound's many books and articles. Cf. also Benjamin Cardozo, *The Nature of the Judicial Process* (New Haven, 1932) pp. 125 ff.
4 Cohen, *op. cit.*, p. 764.
5 *Ibid.*
6 Pound, *Interpretations of Legal History*, pp. 17-18.
7 *Ibid.*, p. 19. "It is noteworthy that the historical school had an instinctive dislike of the period from the end of the sixteenth to the end of the eighteenth century, in which the law was remade under the influence of a creative philosophical theory. . . . Selection of periods for intensive historical study . . . made the interpretation for which the historical school stood an artificial thing, quite out of touch with the actual legal materials to which jurists sought to apply it" (pp. 50, 52).
8 *The Political Testament of Hermann Göring*, a selection of important articles and speeches trans. and arr. by H. W. Blood-Ryan (London, 1939), p. 118.
9 Heinrich von Treitschke, *Politics* (trans. by Blanche W. Dugdale and Torben de Bille, 2 vols., New York, 1916), author's Introduction, p. xxxiii. Gierke shares this view of the importance of Herder's part in the overthrow of the concept of natural law.
10 Cf.: "It is needful to distinguish nicely between the historical school and the historical method. . . . The historical method is the method *par excellence*. Disengaged from every subjective element, it holds to facts and realities, it classifies them and deduces from them the general laws which they permit."—Saleilles, *Le Code Civil et la methode historique*, I, 97, 99, quoted in Pound, "The Scope and Purpose of Sociological Jurisprudence", *Harvard Law Review*, XXV (1911-1912) 153 n.
Although it may be doubted whether the historical method or any method can be "disengaged from every subjective element," and although, regardless of its excellence, it will not make history alone yield the light we need to make decisions regarding principles and beliefs, this remark of Saleilles is cited here to emphasize the distinction between the historical method and the cult of history.
11 Herder, *op. cit.*, XIII, 303.
12 George Anson, *A Voyage Round the World* (Everyman ed.), p. 191.
13 For evidence of the way in which universal ideals may be discredited because they have been too narrowly identified with the interests of one of two contending parties or groups of nations, see the remarkable essay of a German theologian, Ernst Troeltsch, on "The Ideas of Natural Law and Humanity in World Politics," printed in Gierke, *Natural Law and the Theory of Society*, Vol. I.

From another point of view, Troeltsch's essay may also be taken as evidence that it was not entirely fanciful to think that the doctrines fundamental to the Law of Nature were in some sense at stake in the last war (and, presumably he would have agreed, in this war). The failure of the belligerents after the war to view their obligations with sufficient honesty and sufficient intelligence in no way alters this fact.

14 For the background of the "revival" of natural law see J. Charmont, *La Renaissance du droit naturel;* Haines, *The Revival of Natural Law Concepts.* The works of several Continental writers participating in this movement are reprinted in the Modern Legal Philosophy Series.

15 Giorgio del Vecchio, *The Formal Bases of Law* (trans. by John Lisle, Modern Legal Philosophy Series, 1914), p. 8. This volume is a translation of the following works of del Vecchio: *I presuposti filosofici della nozione del diritto* (1905); *Il concetto del diritto* (1906); *Il concetto della natura e il principio del diritto* (1908).

16 *Ibid.,* p. 17.
17 *Ibid.,* p. 16.
18 *Ibid.,* p. 18.
19 *Ibid.,* p. 60.
20 *Ibid.,* p. 62, and n.
21 *Ibid.,* p. 63.
22 *Ibid.,* p. 66.
23 *Ibid.,* p. 69.
24 *Ibid.,* p. 81.
25 *Ibid.,* p. 121.
26 *Ibid.,* p. 125. Cf. pp. 149-53 and, in general, Ch. I of Part II.

27 Rudolf Stammler, *The Theory of Justice* (trans. by Isaac Husik, Modern Legal Philosophy Series, 1925). This volume is a translation of Stammler's *Die Lehre von dem richtigen Rechte* (Berlin, 1902).

28 *Ibid.,* p. 17.
29 *Ibid.,* p. 91.

30 For the formula "natural law with a variable content" (*ein Naturrecht mit wechselndem Inhalte*) see *Wirtschaft und Recht* (1st ed. Leipzig, 1896, 2nd ed. 1906), sec. 33. In the second edition the phrase has been dropped from the title of the section but is retained in the text. It has been frequently repeated—Charmont for example uses it as the title of one of the chapters in *La Renaissance du Droit Naturel*.

31 Stammler is not entirely clear about the nature of his method of just law. In one place he holds that just law is not a norm, is not "the law that we strive to attain in contradistinction to historically given law. Just law is positive law whose content has certain objective qualities" (p. 19). But elsewhere, "Just law need not be at all recognized by positive law. In that case the former is identical with a rule which should take the place of the one actually in force" (p. 53). These two statements are inconsistent. And what of the manifestly untrue assertion that "All positive law is an attempt to be just law" (p. 24)?

32 Stammler, *The Theory of Justice,* p. 107.
33 *Ibid.,* pp. 121-22.

34 *Ibid.*, p. 28.
35 *Ibid.*, pp. 38-39.
36 *Ibid.*, p. 76.
37 *Ibid.*, p. 153.
38 *Ibid.*
39 *Ibid.*, p. 159.
40 *Ibid.*, p. 121.
41 *Ibid.*, p. 161 ff.: "The Principles of Respect. 1. The content of a person's volition must not be made subject to the arbitrary desire of another. 2. Every legal demand must be maintained in such a manner that the person obligated may be his own neighbour.
"The Principles of Participation. 1. A person under a legal obligation must not be arbitrarily excluded from a legal community. 2. Every ability of disposing that is granted by the law may be exclusive only in the sense that the person excluded may be his own neighbour."

NOTES TO CHAPTER V

1 Alfred North Whitehead, *Religion in the Making* (New York, 1926), p. 158.
2 See Grace de Laguna, "Cultural Relativism and Science," *The Philosophical Review*, LI (1942), 141ff.
3 *The Collected Papers of F. W. Maitland* (ed. by H. A. L. Fisher, Cambridge, 1911), I, 121.
4 Cardozo, *The Nature of the Judicial Process*, p. 127.

NOTES TO CHAPTER VI

1 Ralph Waldo Emerson, *Complete Essays and Other Writings* (Modern Library Edition), p. 861.
2 William James, *Some Problems of Philosophy* (New York, 1911), p. 223.
3 U. S. Department of State, *Peace and War, United States Foreign Policy 1931-1941* (U. S. Government Printing Office, Washington, 1942).

INDEX

Adams, John, on American Revolution, 18; and natural law, 19, 132n
Adams, Samuel, 19
American Revolution, 6, 18-19
Anson, George, Lord Anson, *Voyage Round the World,* quoted, 88-89
Antirationalism, in Nazi-Fascist thought, 6, 76; in Vico, 42-47; in Herder, 69-72
Aristotle, 13
Atkinson, Geoffroy, 28, 135n

Bacon, Francis, 34
Barker, Ernest, 19
Becker, Carl, and myth of history, 135n
Biology, influence of on ideas, 48, 53, 54-56, 76; and historical point of view, 31, 57-58, 83; and voyages, 59; in Buffon, 48ff.; in Herder, 57, 59, 63, 74, 76. *See* Nature, concept of; Struggle for existence; Darwin
Blackstone, Sir William, 19, 118
Blumenbach, J. F., 57
Borgese, G. A., 47
Browne, Sir Thomas, 34

Buffon, Georges, comte de, 48-56; and concept of nature, 49-50, 54-55; emphasis on variety, 50, 52; on struggle for existence, 50-51, 55; on man as a species, 49, 51-53; change in idea of species, 53-54, 138n; individual contrasted with species, 53-55; criticism of Linnaeus, 53, 138n; use of voyages, 138n; mentioned, 32, 36, 76, 78, 115
Burlamaqui, J. J., 15, 16, 23

Camper, Pieter, 57, 139n
Cardozo, Benjamin, quoted, 117-118
Chain of being, 57, 58, 62, 65
Charmont, J., and "revival" of natural law, 142n
Cicero, *De Republica,* 14, 15
Cohen, Morris, on rights, 80; criticism of historical school, 83-84
Coke, Sir Edward, 16, 19, 118
Competition. *See* Struggle for existence
Condliffe, J. B., quoted, 124
Consent, doctrine of, in Locke,

17-18; discussed, 22-23, 107-110
Cook, James, effect of his voyages on study of man, 30; 135n, 138n; quoted, 140n
Croce, Benedetto, on Vico, 37-38, 41, 44, 45

Darwin, Charles, impression of savages, 30-31; connects biology and historical point of view, 31, 83; mentioned, 7, 50, 51, 55, 76, 115
Declaration of Independence, 3, 11, 19, 126
De Laguna, Grace, on relativism, 143n
Del Vecchio, Giorgio, 91-95, 96
Democracy, ideas systematically connected, 9; universal in scope, 10; and reason, 107, and unity of thought, 15, 126
Descartes, René, mentioned, 29, 34, 41, 44; on reason, 42
Dickinson, John, 19

Eliot, George, quoted, 75, 105
Ergang, Robert, 63

Fascism, *See* Nazism-Fascism
Ferguson, Adam, on study of mankind in groups, 139-140n
Folk customs, in Vico, 42-43; in Herder, 63, 76
"Fundamental law", 15

Gaius, 14
Geography. *See* Voyages
Goering, Hermann, quoted, 84
Goethe, J. W. von, 47
Grotius, Hugo, on natural law, 15; criticized by Stammler, 99; distinction between Law of Nature and Law of Nations, 134n; and consent, 134n; mentioned, 16, 19, 23, 93
Groups, emphasized in Vico, 48; variation of, 62-63; and study of mankind, 139-140n. *See* Individual

Haines, Charles G., quoted, 13
Haller, Albrecht von, 57
Hegel, G. W. F., 36, 83, 84
Heineccius, J. G., 15, 23; on consent, 134n
Herder, J. G., 56-76; on man as a species, 57; view of history, 56-58, 75-76; on race, 58-59; emphasis on variety, 59, 62, 65; suggestion of inequality, 60-62; influence of biology on, 57; influence of voyages, 61; nationalism, 62-64; relativism, 56, 64-69, 72, 75; on reason, 69-72; on tradition, 70-73; interest in primitive, 72-73; on struggle for existence, 74, 76; knowledge of Vico, 47; mentioned, 30, 32, 84, 85, 87, 115
Historical relativism, described, 35-37. *See* Historicism; History, myth of; Historical school
Historical school, 31, 37, 82ff; criticized by Pound, 84, 141n; strength of, 87; contribution of, 103; influence on del Vecchio, 95; on Stammler, 96. *See* Historicism; History, myth of
Historicism, described, 5-6; reactionary effect, 36-37, 75, 86; and Nazism-Fascism, 35, 77;

and nationalism, 86, 101; in Vico, 37-39, 47-48; in Herder, 56-58, criticized, 82ff; and ideal of justice, 90; and principle of variability, 91, 101; influence, 86-87. See History, myth of

History, myth of, distinguished from historical study, 34, 84-85, 141n; in Hitler, 33-34; in Vico, 34-35; replaced concept of justice, 39; in Germany, 47. See Historicism

Hitler, Adolf, 34, 77; quoted, 138n

Hobbes, Thomas, and Law of Nature, 133n

Hooker, Richard, 16, 23

Human Variable, 8, 32ff. See Groups; Individual; Variability

Hume, David, quoted, 78-79

"Idealists" vs. "realists," 122ff

Individual, value of in democracy, 9; contrasted with species, 53-55, 138n; contrasted with group, 48, 63, 76, 115, 139-140n; in Nazi-Fascist thought, 6, 138n

Ius gentium, associated with natural law, 14; and consent, 134n

Jacobi, F. H., 47

Jefferson, Thomas, 11, 16, 19, 24; quoted, 18

Justice, ideal of, in government, 3, 4, 5, 9, 25, 81; reality of, 20-21, 104-105, 132-133n; intelligibility, 21-22, 105-107; representativeness, 22, 107-110; universality of, 22-24, 93, 110ff; attacks upon, 89-90; and experience, 97, 102, 110, 120; and principle of variability, 26, 113-119; enabling and enfranchising conditions of, 116-119; function of, as a principle, 78-79; 121ff; Montaigne on, 22-23; Pascal on, 133n

Kames, Henry, Lord Kames, 57

Kant, Immanuel, 44, 100; neo-Kantians, 91

Kohn, Hans, 70

Law of Nature, as ideal of justice in government, 3, 4, 5, 9, 25, 81; a set of standards, 25, 81-82, 96-98, 101; a political rather than a legal concept, 25, 80, 97, 131-132n; and democracy, 4, 6, 9, 125-126; development of, 13-19; elements of, 20-27, 103ff.; and principle of variability, 26ff, 91, 113-119; and equality, 4, 13, 17, 116-117, 131n; and mathematics, 5, 20, 29, 133n; and slavery, 12, 19, 112; in American Revolution, 18-19; "revival" of, 91, 142n; authorities on, 132n. See Justice

Layman, point of view of, and principle of consent, 11, 120

Lebensraum, in Malthus, 137n

Levellers, 17

Linnaeus, C., criticized by Buffon, 53, 138n; on man as a species, 137n; mentioned, 57

Locke, John, 16-18; mentioned, 19, 118

Lovejoy, A. O., 36; articles on romanticism, 135n

INDEX

Magna Carta, 15
Maitland, Frederick, quoted, 116
Majority rule, and method of consent, 107-110
Malthus, T. R., and struggle for existence, 137n
Mankind, unity of, 52; in Herder, 56, 58
Meade, G. H., 103
Michelet, Jules, quoted, 39
Milton, John, 118
Minority opinion, and consent, 107-110
Monboddo, James, Lord Monboddo, 57
Montaigne, Michel de, on justice, 22-23, 28-29; mentioned, 30, 110
Myths, in Vico, 45-46; in Sorel, 46; in Herder, 66, 72

National Socialists, 46, 76-77. See Nazism-Fascism
Nationalism, 113, 114, 123; in Herder, 62-64. See Groups; Organismic theory of the state
Nature, Law of. See Law of Nature
Nature, concept of, changes in, 5, 20, 49-50, 55-56, 79; identified with history, 83; as harmony, 20; as strife, See Struggle for existence
Nature, State of, in Locke, 16-17; associated with natural law, 25, 28-29; and economic criticism, 28; in Vico, 43
Nazism-Fascism, ideology, source of, 5-8, 77, 138n. See Groups; Organismic theory; Antirationalism; Nationalism; Hitler

Niebuhr, B. G., acquaintance with Vico, 47; mentioned, 85
Nietzsche, F. W., 7, 73, 77
Noble savage, 30

Omai, 30
Organismic theory of the state, background of, 31, 62, 76-77, 138n
Otis, James, 19, 132n

Pascal, Blaise, on justice, 133n
Plato, 13, 45
Pollock, Sir Frederick, 12
Pope, Alexander, 36
Positive Law, 40, 94; in del Vecchio, 91-92; in Stammler, 98
Pound, Roscoe, on law as "social engineering," 81, 141n; criticism of historical school, 84, 141n
Primitivism, and natural law, 29
Principle of Plenitude, 36, 62, 74, 75
Progress, 37, 41, 62
Pufendorf, Samuel, 15, 16, 23

Race, 58, 59, 60, 63
Réaumur, René A. F. de, 57
Reason, as a value, 21; and emotion, 21, 106-107; in Descartes, 42; in Vico, 42-47; in Herder, 65-66, 69-72. See Justice, intelligibility of
Relativism. See Historical relativism; Biology, influence of; de Laguna, Grace, on cultural relativism
Rights, 79-80, 82; Rights of Man, 25
Romanticism, 26
Rousseau, J. J., quoted, 49

INDEX

Royal Society, The, 57

Savigny, F. K. von, mentioned, 47, 84, 85
Self-determination, and ideal of justice, 87, 90, 124, 141n
Self-interest, 89; validity of, 102-103
Sidney, Algernon, 16
Smith, Adam, 137n
Sociability, 23, 136n
"Social Darwinism," 121
Sorel, Georges, 46; knew *Scienza Nuova*, 136n
Species, idea of, in Buffon, 52-54, 138n; in Herder, 58-59; in Nazi-Fascist thought, 138n; Man as a species, See Buffon, Herder
Spengler, Oswald, 41
Spinoza, Benedict, and Law of Nature, 133n
Staley, Eugene, quoted, 124
Stammler, Rudolph, 91, 95-101; "natural law with a variable content," 95, 98, 142n; method of just law, 142n; principles of just law, 143n
State Department, U. S., 128
State of nature, See Nature, State of
Stein, Heinrich, Freiherr vom, 64
Stoics, and natural law, 3, 13, 104
Struggle for existence, 7, 50-51, 55, 74, 76, 137n, 138n
Swammerdam, Jan, 57

Thomasius, Christian, 16
Totalitarianism, 7
Tradition, 56, 63, 70-73, 76

Travel. *See* Voyages
Treitschke, H. G. von, on Herder and German historical school, 85; mentioned, 77
Tribalism, 64, 66, 72, 90
Troeltsch, E., on natural law, 141-142n
Tyson, Edward, 57

Ulpian, 14
United Nations, 128-129
Universality. *See* Justice

Variability, principle of, omitted from natural law, 26; connection with historicism, 101, 114; and "revival" of natural law, 91; in ideal of justice, 113-119. *See* Buffon; Herder; Human Variable; Variety
Variety, impression of, 8, 26, 113; conflict with universality, 24; and romanticism, 26; and Voyages, 27, 59; in Buffon, 50, 52; in Herder, 59, 62, 65. *See* Variability
Vattel, Emmerich de, 16, 19
Vico, G. B., 34-35, 37-48; and historical relativism, 37-39, 47-48; on natural law, 39-40; influence of travel books on, 42-43; interest in primitive, 41, 43; antirationalism, 42-46; on myths, 45-46; influence in Germany, 47; stress on groups, 48; contribution to historical research, 35, 46; mentioned, 30, 32, 76, 78
Volksgeist, 44, 48, 84, 99
Voyages, influence of, 27-28, 30, 31, 42-43, 59-62, 64, 67, 135n, 138n, 140n

Wagner, Richard, 7
Weber, W. R., translator of *Scienza Nuova*, 47
Wilson, Edmund, on Vico, 34-35
Wilson, James, 19
Wilson, Woodrow, 124
Wolf, F. A., 47
Wolff, Christian, 15, 16, 23
World Society, 4, 90; and community of nations, 121ff. *See* Justice, universality of

NOV 4

DATE DUE